The Heart of Krishna

SRI GURU GAURANGAU JAYATAH!

Bhakti Siddhanta Vani

THE HEART OF KRISHNA

VAISHNAVA APARADH & THE PATH OF SPIRITUAL CAUTION

REVISED EDITION

OM VISHNUPADA
PARAMAHAMSA PUJYAPADA
VAISHNAVA SARVABHAUMA SRI
BHAKTI PROMODE PURI
GOSWAMI MAHARAJ

MANDALA
publishing group

Published for
Bhakti Siddhanta Vani

by the
Mandala Publishing Group
2240-B 4th Street, San Rafael, CA 94901
phone: 415 460 6112 fax: 415 460 5218
mandala@mandala.org www.mandala.org

ISBN: 1-886069-47-6

The publishers would like to express their deep gratitude to the following persons without whose help this publication would not have been possible:

Financial Contribution:
Govardhana Das

Editing & Proofreading:
Jaya Sri, Kalimba Goravani, Sreed Haran, Jill Tabler, Vidagdha Madhava Prabhu.
Special thanks to Sri Sarvabhavana Das, who translated the original Bengali into English.
Special thanks to Jagadananda Das & Jagadish Das for all the corrections and additions to this revised edition.

Graphic Design: Room 19 & MDG

Readers interested in the subject matter may also contact:

Gopinath Gaudiya Maths in India

Ishodyan, Sri Mayapur
District Nadia, West Bengal
Phone: 91-347-245-307

Chakratirtha Road
Jagannath Puri, Orissa
Phone: 91-6752-25690

Old Dauji Mandhir
Gopeswara Road
Vrindavan, U.P. 281121
Phone: 91-565-444-185

Printed in China through Palace Press International

Contents

Jagad Guru Srila Prabhupada Bhaktisiddhanta Saraswati Goswami Thakur

Sri Guru Gaurangau Jayatah

INTRODUCTION

THE SANSKRIT WORD FOR "OFFENSE" (*aparādha*) is explained etymologically as *rādhād arthād ārādhanād apagataḥ,* "to be distanced from worship." Offenses committed at the lotus feet of Vaishnavas, the devotees, distance one from devotional service to the Supreme Lord. But in a higher sense, it means to be removed from the service of Sri Radha. All divine service to Krishna is being conducted under her direction. To offend her servitors is to make one unfit for her divine service. The whole aim of Krishna consciousness is *rādhā-dāsyam*, the divine service of Sri Radha, and offenses at the lotus feet of Vaishnavas make one unfit for such service.

The Lord is overly protective of his devotees (*bhakta-vatsala*). He cannot tolerate any offenses against them. They have bhakti (devotion), and they can awaken it within us. Bhakti is the sole means to attract Krishna, who is a slave of devotion. The same is true of Sri Chaitanya Mahaprabhu. The *Chaitanya Bhāgavata* states: "A person can attain the shelter of Mahaprabhu only by the grace of a higher Vaishnava. Religious practices and even chanting the Holy Name without devotion is useless."

Srila Bhaktisiddhanta Saraswati Prabhupada writes in his commentary: "Without developing a spirit of service, chanting the Holy Name is in vain. A natural desire to engage in service can only awaken in the heart when one receives the blessings of an unalloyed devotee." Here, "a natural desire to engage in service" is the definition of bhakti.

In the following verse, Vrindavan Das Thakur goes on to say: "If a person commits an offense at the lotus feet of a Vaishnava, even though he may have received Krishna's mercy, he will never attain divine love, prema."

Srila Prabhupada writes: "One who commits offenses to a Vaishnava becomes incapable of rendering pure devotion because he is committing offenses to the Holy Name. Although it may appear that such an offender is still being shown favor by the Lord as he continues to make a show of chanting without difficulty, the Lord is in fact very displeased with him because of his antagonism toward devotees. Therefore, in any discussion of *nāmāparādha,* it is always stressed that we must first give up *sādhu-nindā* or finding fault with devotees."

Regarding the phrase *kṛṣṇa-kṛpā hoile-o* ("even though he may have received Krishna's mercy") in Vrindavan Das's verse quoted above, it is apparent that Srila Saraswati Thakur considers that an offender to the Vaishnavas is only making a pretense of chanting. Seeing him, people may think the Lord still favors him, but they are wrong. The Lord is not even slight-

Advaita Acharya

Nityananda Avadhuta

Sri Chaitanya Deva

ly moved by their sham devotion."

The author of *Chaitanya Bhāgavata*, Vrindavan Das Thakur, says that these statements are not his alone; they are the verdict of the Vedas. Srila Bhaktisiddhanta Saraswati Thakur did not tolerate any disrespect towards genuine Vaishnavas. Similarly, Sri Chaitanya Mahaprabhu also emphatically denounced any failure to show Vaishnava devotees the respect that is their due.

To understand the seriousness of Vaishnava aparadh, or offenses to devotees, one must grasp the multi-faceted, multi-dimensional nature of the Supreme Personality of Godhead, Sri Krishna Chaitanya Mahaprabhu. Lord Chaitanya appears in six aspects. He himself is the source of all incarnations in Kali Yuga and the savior of all souls. He is Krishna, the son of Maharaj Nanda, fully enriched with the mood and radiance of Sri Radha. In the same way that Mahaprabhu is Krishna, Nityananda Prabhu is Balaram, Krishna's *prakāśa-vigraha*. Balaram is the second member of the original *catur-vyūha* in Dvaraka (Vasudeva, Balaram, Pradyumna and Aniruddha), whose expansion in Vaikuntha is Sankarshan. Sankarshan's partial expansion is Mahavishnu, who lies in the causal ocean for the sake of Krishna. This Mahavishnu appears in Chaitanya lila as Advaita Acharya. What is left of Sri Radhika after Krishna has plundered her emotions and luster is Sri Gadadhara Pandit. Mahaprabhu's energies are Sri Gadadhara Pandit, Svarupa Damodar, Ramananda Raya and others. His devotees are led by Srivasa Thakur, who is Sri Narada Muni in Krishna lila. The final aspect of Chaitanya Mahaprabhu's six-fold manifestation consists of the two kinds of spiritual masters — the one who initiates the disciple in the spiritual path and the one who instructs him.

Gadadhara Pundit

Srivas Thakur

The slightest disregard to any one of these six aspects of the Lord is equal to disregarding the Supreme Lord Sri Chaitanya Mahaprabhu himself. Therefore Srila Krishna Das Kaviraj Goswami offers prayers to all of these manifestations in the very first verse of the *Chaitanya Charitāmṛta*:

vande gurūn īśa-bhaktān
īśān īśāvatārakān
tat-prakāśāṁs ca tac-chaktīḥ
kṛṣṇa-caitanya-saṁjñakaṁ

"I offer my obeisances unto both the instructing and initiating spiritual masters, the devotees led by Srivasa, the Lord's avatars led by Advaita Prabhu, his expansions like Nityananda, his shaktis (energies) led by Gadadhara Pandit, and the primeval lord himself, Sri Krishna Chaitanya."

(*Chaitanya Charitāmṛta, Ādi* 1.1)

In the beginning of the second chapter of the *Antya-līlā* of the *Śrī Chaitanya Charitāmṛta*, Srila Krishna Das Kaviraj offers the following invocatory prayers (*maṅgalācaraṇa*) to the same six truths, as well as to Krishna along with his beloved Radha and her girl-friends led by Lalita and Visakha. In so doing, he shows special veneration for the Vaishnavas:

vande'haṁ śrī-guroḥ śrī-yuta-pada-kamalaṁ
śrī-gurūn vaiṣṇavāṁś ca
śrī-rūpaṁ sāgrajātaṁ saha-gaṇa-raghunā-
thānvitaṁ taṁ sa-jīvam
sādvaitam savadhutaṁ parijana-sahitaṁ
kṛṣṇa-caitanya-devaṁ
śrī-rādhā-kṛṣṇa-pādān saha-gaṇa-lalitā-
śrī-viśākhānvitāṁś ca

"I offer my obeisances unto the lotus feet of my Guru (both my initiating and teacher on the path of devotion), to all the preceptors in the disciplic succession and to all the Vaishnavas. I offer my obeisances to Sri Rupa Goswami, his elder brother Sanatan, his other associates headed by Sri Raghunath Das, and Sri Jiva. I further offer my obeisances to Sri Krishna Chaitanya Mahaprabhu along with Advaita Acharya, Nityananda Avadhuta and all his other associates. And finally, I offer my obeisances to the lotus feet of Sri Radha and Sri Krishna, along with all the gopis headed by Lalita and Visakha."

(*Chaitanya Charitāmṛta, Antya-līlā* 2.1)

Kaviraj Goswami writes further:

"Before beginning the narration of the pastimes of Sri Chaitanya Mahaprabhu, I invoke the benediction of Sri Guru, the Vaishnavas and the Divinity, simply by meditating on them. Such meditation destroys all detriments on the spiritual path, and helps one to fulfill all their desires."

(*Chaitanya Charitāmṛta Ādi* 11.10)

Srila Bhaktivinode Thakur

We must note very carefully that the Vaishnavas have been included within the full conception of Divinity. Krishna Das Kaviraj not only invoked their blessings at the very beginning of his biography of Sri Chaitanya Mahaprabhu, but went on to glorify them throughout this master work. He describes the Vaishnavas' extraordinary qualities and the spiritual benefit resulting from serving them. He also makes several warnings regarding the disastrous effects of Vaishnava aparadh, stating for example:

"If a devotee commits Vaishnava aparadh, his offense is like a mad elephant uprooting and trampling his creeper of devotion; afterwards the creeper's leaves dry up and become lifeless."

(*Chaitanya Charitāmṛta, Madhya* 19.156)

Krishna Das describes three categories of Vaishnavas — *kaniṣṭha* (neophyte), *madhyama* (intermediate) and *uttama* (advanced). He further states that to gain shelter of a Vaishnava it is imperative to first receive the mercy of Nityananda Prabhu. In the following passage, he describes the characteristics of the *uttama* devotees that he personally knew:

"All of the Vaishnavas who live in Vrindavan are absorbed in singing the all-auspicious name of Sri Krishna. Sri Mahaprabhu and Nityananda are their life and soul. They know nothing but devotion to Sri Radha and Krishna. My shelter at the Vaishnavas' lotus feet has been granted only by the mercy of Nityananda Prabhu."

(*Chaitanya Charitāmṛta, Ādi* 5.228-30)

Srila Bhaktisiddhanta Saraswati Prabhupada highlights these characteristics in his *Anubhāṣya*: "All the Vaishnavas living in the holy dhama of Sri Vrindavan are completely devoted to the all-auspicious holy name of Krishna and have taken shelter of the path of devotion, primarily by glorifying the Lord. Sriman Mahaprabhu and Nityananda are their life and soul. They accept no illegitimate forms of devotion; all they know is the eternal service of Sri Radha and Sri Krishna."

Srila Bhaktivinoda Thakur, a *nitya-siddha* (eternal associate) of the Lord, instructs us to pray to Mahaprabhu in order to get the association of pure devotees. When we find shelter in the shade of a Vaishnava's lotus feet, we should shed tears of remorse with total humility, submitting to him the plight of our material existence, which is the result of turning away from Krishna. The Vaishnava is an ocean of compassion and feels the pain of others. When he pleads on our behalf to the Lord, Krishna responds and kindly accepts us as the followers of his favorites. Krishna's mercy descends only through the Vaishnavas.

There is Krishna and there is *kārṣṇa*. Krishna's mercy is embodied in pure devotees, who are known as *kārṣṇa*. The lotus feet of a Vaishnava guru represent the mercy of the Lord. Krishna is the priceless treasure enthroned in the Sri Guru's heart. The Lord can easily give this treasure to those who are surrendered to his devotees. There is no other way to receive Krishna's grace than to serve and take shelter at the lotus feet of a Vaishnava.

Srila Kaviraj Goswami discusses the importance of honoring the Vaishnava's remnants, using the example of Sri Kali Das, the uncle of Raghunath Das Goswami:

"Taking the food remnants of Vaishnavas is so potent it forced Mahaprabhu to give his mercy to Kali Das. Don't hesitate. Eat the Vaishnava's remnants and you will fulfill your heart's desire."

"Food offered to Krishna is called maha prasad. After maha prasad has been taken by a devotee, his remnants are glorified as maha maha prasad. The dust of a pure devotee's feet, the water of his foot-bath and his food remnants are three extremely potent spiritual substances. By honoring these three, one will be filled with ecstatic love for Krishna. All the scriptures declare this again and again. My dear devotees! Please hear me: believe in these three and honor them in a mood of service, and you will achieve the purpose of your existence — ecstatic love of Krishna. This is the greatest mercy of Krishna, and Kali Das is living proof."
(*Antya-līlā* 16.57-63)

Srila Bhaktivinoda Thakur has also written:

"When will Mahaprabhu shower his mercy upon me so I may have shelter in the shade of the Vaishnava's lotus feet? I will humbly stand before him, giving up all pretension. Holding a straw between my teeth and weeping, I will tell him of my miserable existence. I will admit that my life is one never-ending misery and beg him to put an end to all of my suffering. The kind Vaishnava will beg Sri Krishna with all his might. Then Krishna, moved by the Vaishnava's sincerity, will shower me with his divine grace." (*Kalyāṇa-kalpa-taru*)

"O Vaishnava Thakur, you are an Ocean of Mercy. Please shower your compassion upon me. Give me the shade of your lotus feet and purify my polluted heart. I am following you, begging. Krishna is yours, you have the power give Him to me!"

Saranagati

In another song, Srila Bhaktivinoda writes:

"O Vaishnava Thakur, you are an ocean of mercy. Please shower your compassion upon me. Give me the shade of your lotus feet and purify my polluted heart. Sri Krishna is yours and you have the power to give him to me! Knowing this, I am following you like a beggar, appealing for your mercy." (*Śaraṇāgati*)

Narottama Das Thakur glorifies the Vaishnavas with great enthusiasm in both his *Prārthanā* and *Prema-bhakti-candrikā*:

"I am so sinful; how can I possibly serve the Lord? I have no love for either my guru or the devotees. Constantly deluded by the unlimited illusory energy, I have not developed the least bit of affection for the Vaishnavas. Day and night, I am blinded by my desire for the sense objects. The witch Maya is waiting to hang a noose around my neck. I have no power to resist her on my own. I am helpless without your mercy. I know that you never see the faults of anyone, so I am begging you — please save me." (*Prārthanā*)

Sri Krishna Chaitanya Mahaprabhu

Narottama's songs are filled with wonderful glorification of Vaishnavas. All devotees treasure them as priceless instructions for increasing one's devotion. From his childhood, Srila Bhaktisiddhanta Prabhupada chose Narottama's songbook as his constant companion on the path of devotion.

Vrindavan Das Thakur considered himself to be the last direct servant of Nityananda Prabhu. He has uninhibitedly glorified the Vaishnavas throughout his masterpiece, *Chaitanya Bhāgavata*. In the invocation to this book, he first glorifies Sri Chaitanya and Nityananda in four Sanskrit verses. Then in the first Bengali couplet, he writes:

"I first offer my unlimited obeisances at the feet of Sri Krishna Chaitanya's dearest associates, the devotees. And then I pray to him, who appeared in Nabadwip and was also known as Visvambhara."

Sri Vrindavan Das then explains why he first offers humble obeisances to Mahaprabhu's devotees before offering them to Mahaprabhu himself. He explains: "The Supreme Lord has boldly declared in all the scriptures that 'The worship of my devotees is higher than worshipping me.' By first glorifying the Vaishnavas, I am guaranteed success in writing my book."

Vrindavan Das is here referring to a statement made by Krishna to Uddhava in the *Śrīmad Bhāgavatam* — *mat-pūjābhyadhikā* (11.19.21).

Subsequently, Vrindavan Das goes on to glorify Nityananda Prabhu, saying that only by his mercy is it possible for one to glorify Chaitanya Mahaprabhu.

In the *Itihāsa-samuccaya*, it is said that if one wishes to receive the blessings of the Supreme Lord, he should attempt first to please the devotees. The smiling face of the Lord shines on those who have been successful in satisfying the Vaishnavas.

The following verse, from the *Pautrāyaṇa-Śruti*, is quoted in Srila Madhvacharya's commentary to the Vedanta Sutra (3.3.47):

"Worship the devotees, serve them and hear from them; they will protect you."

Similarly, Sri Baladeva Vidyabhushan quotes the following verse from the *Muṇḍaka-upaniṣad* (3.1.10) in his *Govinda-Bhāṣya* commentary on the Vedanta Sutra (3.3.51):

"If you want a real treasure (*bhūti*) you must serve one who knows the Self (*ātmajñam*)." Baladeva explains that "one who truly knows the Self" is a devotee. The "real treasure" spoken of means everything up to and including liberation.

The following important verse in the *Śrīmad Bhāgavatam* also explains the importance of associating with devotees:

jñāne prayāsam udapāsya namanta eva
jivanti san-mukharitāṁ bhavadīya-vārtām
sthāne sthitāḥ śruti-gatāṁ tanu-vāṇ-manobhir
ye prāyaśo' jita jito'py asi tais tri-lokyām

Brahma prayed to Krishna, "My dear Lord, those who have given up abstract thinking and armchair philosophizing, remain constantly in the association of devotees in order to hear your glories, and begin divine service with their body, mind, and words. Although you are unconquerable and rarely attained, you are conquered by them."
(*Śrīmad Bhāgavatam* 10.14.3)

In the *Padma-purāṇa*, Shiva says to his wife Parvati:

"O Goddess, higher than the worship of all the gods and goddesses is the worship of the Supreme Lord Vishnu. But higher still is the worship of everyone and everything that is dear to him, including Ganga Devi, Tulasi Devi, the book *Bhāgavata* and the devotee *Bhāgavata*."

Vrindavan Das cautions us against seeing Vaishnavas externally. Such superficial vision is condemned:

"In order to teach us the absurdity of judging devotees externally according to race, color, family, or other considerations, the Supreme Lord arranged for Hari Das Thakur to take birth in the lowest section of society. All the scriptures emphasize that if a pure devotee appears even in the lowest social circumstances, he is still to be worshipped by everyone.

"The person who thinks of a Vaishnava in terms of his bodily designations is most sinful. He will be born repeatedly in the lowest forms of life.

"A Vaishnava may appear in any family or section of society, yet he is still the most elevated person by the decree of the scriptures."

God is the protector of all living entities, and he cannot tolerate insults and disrespect shown to his devotees. Extremely mindful of his dear devotees' well-being, he refuses to accept any worship from those who slight them. The Lord loves his devotees so much that he not only accepts food and gifts from them, but sometimes he even steals their offerings! On the other hand, he is repulsed by offerings from a non-devotee.

In one pastime, Krishna was very eager to eat plain chipped rice cooked by Vidura's wife and ignored a royal feast set by Duryodhana. Similarly the Lord could not resist eating the few morsels of flat rice offered by Sudama. He told him:

"O Brahmin! What wonderful things have you brought for me from your home? Even a small offering from a devotee is a grand feast for me, whereas a non-devotee's feast cannot satisfy me in the least. Anything offered to me with love, I accept with love."

(*Śrīmad Bhāgavatam* 10.81.3-4)

"A person may learn all the Vedas, but if he has no devotion, how can he be my devotee? Whereas if a person born into the lowest section of society has devotion, he is very dear to me. All respect must be given to such an elevated soul. His offerings must be accepted by all, for he is as much worthy of worship as I am."

Mahaprabhu himself states this in the *Chaitanya Charitāmṛta*, quoting from the *Itihāsa-samuccaya*:

"I have no great love for a Brahmin knowledgeable in all the four Vedas who is not my devotee, whereas a devoted untouchable outcaste is very dear to me. You should give such a devotee gifts and should accept the food that he offers you. He is as worshipable as I myself."

(*Madhya* 19.50)

Mahaprabhu also quotes *Hari-bhakti-sudhodaya* (3.11-12):

"An outcaste who is clean and whose sinful activities have been burnt to ashes by the powerful fire of Krishna bhakti should no longer be considered in terms of his caste. Intelligent people will praise him, while they will deride the Vedic scholar who is an atheist. Anyone devoid of devotion may take birth in a great family or nation, have extensive knowledge of the scriptures, perform austerities, or chant Vedic mantras, but such things are like ornaments on a dead body. Only fools will be impressed."

Once, when Mahaprabhu went to embrace him, Hari Das objected with all humility, saying:

"My dear Lord, please do not touch me. I am most fallen, the lowest of men."

Mahaprabhu replied: "I want to touch you just to purify myself. You are so pure, it is as if at every moment you are bathing in all the sacred rivers, visiting all the holy places of pilgrimage, and performing every sacrifice, austerity, and charity imaginable. You are more exalted than any Brahmin or sannyasi." (*Madhya* 11.188-191)

The Lord then recited this sloka from the *Śrīmad Bhāgavatam* (3.33.7) to support his statements:

aho bata śvapaco'to garīyān
yaj-jihvāgre vartate nāma tubhyam
tepus tapas te juhuvuḥ sasnur āryā
brahmānūcur nāma gṛṇanti ye te

"O Lord! Those on whose tongues your name is present are the topmost members of human society, even if they belong to the untouchable classes. Anyone who chants your name must already have performed all austerities and sacrifices, bathed in all the holy rivers and mastered the Vedas. In short, he has all the noble qualities of the Aryan."

In the *Padma-purāṇa, Uttara-khaṇḍa*, it is declared:

"When a person is admitted into Vishnu's family, he is called a Vaishnava. It has been said that of all the divisions of human society, the Vaishnava is certainly the most exalted." The *Dvārakā-mahātmya* states:

"A person who is devoted to Janardana, the Supreme Personality of Godhead, is a saint even if he is born into a low-class family; whereas if a person is born into an aristocratic family of noble lineage and is not a devotee of the Lord, he is equal to the meat-eating outcastes."

It is therefore prohibited to associate with non-Vaishnavas or with so-called Brahmins who have no devotion for the Lord and are inimical to those who do. This is stated in the *Padma-purāṇa*:

"The association of meat-eaters is strictly prohibited because their lifestyle goes against scriptural regulations; in the same manner, contact with a non-Vaishnava Brahmin must be avoided. On the other hand, a Vaishnava — one who is initiated and is affectionate to the Lord and his devotees — is capable of purifying all three worlds, even if born into a low-class family. What is the need of stating this repeatedly? One should avoid conversation or physical contact with a non-devotee Brahmin, even by error."

Sri Balaramaji

Vrindavan Das also supports this by saying,

"Scriptures forbid us to touch such so-called Brahmins, or to talk to them, or even to offer them respect. If one talks to someone who though born a Brahmin is not a Vaishnava, then all the benefits of his good works are lost."
(*Chaitanya Bhāgavata Ādi* 16.302, 305)

According to the *Padma-purāṇa*, the characteristics of a Vaishnava are as follows:

"One who has received initiation into a Vishnu mantra and is dedicated to worshipping Vishnu is classified as a Vaishnava by spiritual preceptors; all others are non-Vaishnavas." (*Hari-bhakti-vilāsa* 1.55)

Those who are simply born into a Brahmin family but

are non-Vaishnavas, and who are inimical towards Vishnu and Vaishnavas, are condemned. Vrindavan Das decries such pretentious Brahmins, citing Shiva's words in the *Varāha-purāṇa*:

"In Kali Yuga, demons will be born in Smarta Brahmin families to harass and torture the righteous devotees of the Lord. The demons choose Kali Yuga to be born in so they can torment those rare persons who adhere to the path enunciated by the Vedas (Sruti). They viciously attempt to disrupt the devotees' service to the Supreme Lord."

These Brahmin imposters view Vaishnavas who have a bad background with contempt. They scoff when they see them engage in spiritual practices like hearing and chanting or receiving honor and respect. They vainly try to expose such a Vaishnava's background and other mundane trivialities in order to tarnish his reputation. The *Bṛhad-āraṇyaka Upanisad* (3.9.10) describes them, saying:

Srila Bhakti Promode Puri Maharaja

"One who leaves the world fully understanding the Absolute Truth is honored as a Brahmin, but one who does not has wasted his life."

Krishna Das Kaviraj prohibits seeing not only God's form, but that of his devotees also, as mundane. "There is no greater blasphemy than to think that the body of Vishnu is material."

(*Chaitanya Charitāmṛta Ādi* 7.155)

And Mahaprabhu says: "The Vaishnava's body is never mundane; it is supramundane and supercharged with ecstasy."

(*Chaitanya Charitāmṛta Antya* 4.191)

It may be asked why Mahaprabhu calls the devotee's body supramundane. In response to this, Kaviraj Goswami says:

"At the time of diksha (initiation), the devotee surrenders to Krishna with body and soul. In reciprocation, Krishna accepts him, elevating him, body and soul, to a status equal to his own (*ātma-sama*). The Lord transforms the Vaishnava's body and makes it a repository of transcendental emotions."

(*Chaitanya Charitāmṛta, Antya* 8.192-193)

Srila Krishna Das Kaviraj explains further why a pure Vaishnava's body is *aprākṛta*, or supramundane, quoting the *Śrīmad Bhāgavatam*: "When people reject materialism and surrender to me, conducting their lives under my direction, they attain immortality. They become eligible to be with me and share spiritual emotions (*rasa*) with me in their spiritual identity."

(*Śrīmad Bhāgavatam* 11.29.34)

But what is meant by surrender? Krishna Das Kaviraj writes:

"Although one who has completely renounced the world (*akiñcana*) and one who is completely sheltered in Krishna (*śaraṇāgata*) may appear to be the same externally, the devotee who has given up the world has also offered his soul. As soon as one takes shelter and surrenders himself to Krishna, the Lord makes him the same as Himself (*ātma-sama*)."

(*Chaitanya Charitāmṛta, Madhya* 22.96,99)

Srīla Prabhupada Bhaktisiddhanta Saraswati Thakur comments on these verses in his *Anubhāṣya* commen-

Govinda, lover of the cows

tary: "At the time of initiation, the devotee gives up material conceptions and starts to think in terms of *sambandha-jñāna* or his eternal relationship with Krishna and His family. As soon as he has this supramundane or spiritual knowledge, he becomes eligible to serve the Lord in a similarly spiritual identity. As soon as the surrendered devotee is free from the shelter of Maya, Krishna adopts him and makes him His own. At this stage, the devotee's delusion as enjoyer of material pleasures dissipates, and his real self merges with his new identity an eternal servant of Krishna. The devotee attains his spiritual body (*sac-cid-ānanda-svarūpa*) and his eternal service to Krishna, serving Him in his own transcendental form. The pure devotee's ecstatic service is an elevated stage of devotion that is often misinterpreted and misunderstood by those unacquainted with the science of devotion. For this kind of aparadh one is deprived of the shelter of a Vaishnava guru."

(*Anubhāṣya*, *Chaitanya Charitāmṛta*, *Antya* 4.193)

Mahaprabhu taught everyone that a Vaishnava's transcendental body is unlike that of an ordinary person, or even an extraordinary person. The Lord did not view personalities like Hari Das Thakur, who took birth in a low-class family, or Sanatan Goswami, whose body was diseased, or Vasudeva Vipra, who was suffering from acute leprosy, as social outcasts or disease-ridden beggars. Instead he embraced them, proving that a pure devotee's body is never impure.

Srila Prabhupada explains, "By embracing these devotees, Gaurasundara was trying to show all his followers that a pure devotee's body is transcendental. Unlike the bodies of the fruitive workers and philosophers who are filled with other desires, the pure devotee's body is not material, i.e., it is not dedicated to sense enjoyment. When we say the devotee has a spiritual body, we mean that it is fit for Krishna's service and filled with transcendental feeling and therefore permeated with eternity, knowledge and bliss." (*Anubhāṣya* to *Antya* 4.191)

The use of the term *ātma-sama* in the above verses from the *Chaitanya Charitāmṛta* does not imply that the devotees are equal to the Supreme Lord in every respect. The Supreme Lord is the only one who possesses transcendental qualities to an infinite degree. The jiva can only possess these qualities to a finite degree.

Mahaprabhu says: "The finite and the Infinite can never be considered equal, just as a tiny spark is never equal to a blazing fire."

The following verse from the *Sarvajña-sūkta* is found in the *Bhāgavat-sandarbha* and also in Sridhara Swami's commentary to the *Śrīmad Bhāgavatam* (1.7.6):

"The Supreme Lord is the embodiment of eternality, knowledge, and bliss. Two of his multifarious spiritual energies are: *hlādinī śakti*, the pleasure-giving potency, and *saṁvit*, perfect knowledge of the self and all other things, while the jivas are cocooned in ignorance, and deeply anchored in suffering."

Only by taking complete shelter of Sri Radhika and her serving group, the *hlādinī śakti*, can we realize our innate spiritual identity and render service to the holy lotus feet of Sri Guru, Gauranga and Krishna.

As the Lord himself says:

"The foolish person who thinks that the individual soul and the Supreme Lord are the same in every respect is a heretic, punishable by the god of death."

(*Chaitanya Charitāmṛta Madhya* 18.113)

This is confirmed by the *Vaiṣṇava-tantra*:

"One who considers gods like Brahma and Rudra to be equal to Narayan is considered to be a heretic."

mad-bhakta-pūjyābhyadhikā sarva-bhūteṣu man-matiḥ

"The worship of my devotees is the real worship of me. In fact it is higher than worshipping my very self."

My dear devotees, please read and listen carefully to the divine stories and instructions that follow, and pray to the Supreme Lord and his devotees — the Vaishnavas — that we may always worship and adore them and thereby enter *The Heart of Krishna*.

The Vaishnava King
AMBARISH MAHARAJ

WE OFTEN HEAR DEVOTEES LAMENT, "Why is it that I have no taste for chanting the Holy Name (*kṛṣṇa-nāma*)?" Krishna Das Kaviraj Goswami answers this question in the eighth chapter of the *Ādi-līlā* of *Śrī Chaitanya Charitāmṛta*. If we want to sincerely absorb ourselves in bhajan, we must take his instructions seriously. Srila Bhaktivinoda Thakur summarizes these instructions in the following way:

"The eighth chapter describes the glories of Chaitanya Mahaprabhu and Nityananda Prabhu. One can chant the Holy Name birth after birth, but if one is chanting with offenses (*nāmāparādha*), he will never develop love for Krishna. This means that an offensive chanter who exhibits symptoms of ecstasy (*aṣṭa-sāttvika-vikāra*) is a fraud. However, one who repeats the names of Mahaprabhu, Nityananda Prabhu, and the Pancha Tattva in full surrender will be freed from aparadhs by the mercy of the Pancha Tattva, and will then experience growing love for the Holy Name and for Krishna."

Srila Krishna Das Kaviraj writes: "The learned speech of pandits who do not accept the Pancha Tattva is like the croaking of frogs. Those who do not accept the Pancha Tattva but worship Krishna get neither Krishna's mercy nor the supreme destination. They are like Jarasandha and other kings who previously followed the Vedic religion and worshiped Vishnu but did not recognize Krishna. Because they did not accept Krishna's divinity they were considered to be demons. Similarly those who do not accept the divinity of Sri Chaitanya Mahaprabhu are called demons."

(*Chaitanya Charitāmṛta Ādi* 8.6-9)

Bhaktivinoda Thakur explains in his *Amṛta-pravāha-bhāṣya*: "One who does not recognize the Pancha Tattva, although culturing devotion, can never attract Krishna's mercy."

How can anyone who rejects the teachings of Gauranga Mahaprabhu possibly understand the meaning of devotion? This is why Jarasandha's example has been given. Srila Prabhupada Bhaktisiddhanta Saraswati has written in his *Anubhāṣya* to that verse:

"Jarasandha and others like him abandoned the service to Krishna because they did not recognize him as the source of Vishnu and other forms of the Divine. They even went so far as to criticize and hate Krishna. Thus though they may have worshiped Lord Vishnu with the Vedic mantras, these acts of worship are considered demonic. In the same way, if one neglects the eternal duty of the atomic spark of consciousness, service to Lord Chaitanya, then his worship of Vishnu is nothing but a disturbance and cannot be considered true Vaishnavism."

Lord Chaitanya Mahaprabhu is the combined form of Radha and Krishna. He is therefore ontologically identical with them. The Lord himself appears as a devotee and shows the perfection of devotion by his example.

What is the need for the Supreme Lord to take the renounced order of life? His idea was that people would offer him respect as a monk, and that by so doing their sufferings would be alleviated. Therefore Krishna Das Kaviraj states with great emotion,

"Anyone who does not worship this compassionate Lord may be virtuous in every respect, but he is still considered a demon. Therefore I lift my arms in the air and implore you to worship Lord Chaitanya and Nityananda, discarding your doubts and arguments. If some logician says that the truth can be established through reason, and that he will worship the form of the Lord that is established by rational argument, then to him I answer: Just consider the blessings of Sri Krishna Chaitanya! I promise you that you will be astonished if you examine his compassion carefully."

(*Chaitanya Charitāmṛta Ādi* 8.12-15)

Srila Prabhupada gives an extensive commentary on these verses in his *Anubhāṣya*. We will simply give a summary here. "Normally, rationalists base their philosophy on direct perception and inference. It is important to state that perceptions and arguments based on a *priori* knowledge received through disciplic succession can elucidate the Supreme Truth. Normally, however, the conditioned soul cannot establish the nature of the Absolute through his sense perceptions, which are based a *priori* on a ignorance of that truth. However, if some fortunate jiva who has been blessed with a perception of higher truth examines Lord Chaitanya's mercy without bias, then through a comparison with every kind of blessing, he will be able to conclude that never have such gifts of mercy been given by anyone, not by anyone within or without the creation, nor by any incarnation of God, nay, not even by Krishna himself! The supreme blessings given by Sri Chaitanya Mahaprabhu are truly a thing of wonder and amazement."

Anyone who does not follow the teachings of Lord Chaitanya may be engaged for many lifetimes in the practices of devotion, hearing and chanting about the Lord, but he will never attain the treasure of prema.

bahu janme kare jadi śravaṇa kīrtana
tabu ta nā pāya kṛṣṇa pade prema dhana

(*Chaitanya Charitāmṛta Ādi* 8.16)

Prabhupada writes, "If anyone engages in hearing and chanting and other devotional activities without taking shelter of Mahaprabhu, then there is no possibility of attaining prema, though he tries for many lifetimes."

According to Mahaprabhu's teachings: "Only one who is humble, tolerant of others, and treats others respectfully while expecting nothing in return can escape the clutches of the ten offenses. Their very lives are situated in *kṛṣṇa-nāma* and divine love of God."

Bhaktivinoda Thakur also comments that if one engages in hearing and chanting while committing the ten offenses to the Holy Name, he will not attain divine love for Krishna.

To illustrate the gravity of Vaishnava aparadh, the first of the ten *nāmāparādhas*, the story of Ambarish Maharaj and Durvasa Muni from the *Śrīmad Bhāgavatam* is especially helpful.

Vaivasvata Sraddha Deva was the seventh Manu of the seventh Manvantara, approximately halfway into the life cycle of the universe according to Vedic time calculation. His son was Nabhaga and his grandson Nābhāga. Nābhāga's son was the exalted pure devotee Ambarish, whose purity could ward off even the inescapable curse of a Brahmin.

> *"I am completely under the control of my devotees. I have no freedom. I live happily within their hearts. Even those who are devotees of My devotees are very dear to Me."*

Ambarish Maharaj was an extremely fortunate soul. He ruled over the entire Earth and was the proprietor of inexhaustible wealth, yet he treated his material possessions with disdain. Having cultivated deep love for the Lord and his devotees, he looked upon the world and all its allurements as trash.

Ambarish Maharaj completely absorbed his entire being, within and without, in Krishna. The lotus feet of Krishna were ever present within his pure mind. His voice was filled with Krishna katha. He cleansed his soul by cleaning the temple. His ears continuously drank the nectar of Krishna katha, and his eyes were filled with beautiful visions of the Deities. The only aromas he knew were of Tulasi, incense, and flowers offered to Krishna. He relished food tasted by Krishna; he walked to and from the temple and holy places. Ambarish Maharaj's entire being was saturated with Krishna consciousness. His only motive was to please Krishna. And anyone who saturates their body, mind, senses, and words in the Lord's service as he did will develop deep attraction to the Lord and his pure devotees.

The ministers and Brahmins who were the King's well-wishers advised Ambarish Maharaj on running the affairs of his empire. The emperor did not personally perform any religious rituals, but left them to be done by the most dedicated Brahmins. He kept aloof so that he could immerse himself in devotion to the Supreme Lord. Sri Hari, being extremely pleased with Ambarish's devotion, gave him the protection of his Sudarshan chakra, who is always ready to shield the Lord's devotees from harm. Sudarshan was thus always by Ambarish's side.

To satisfy Krishna, Ambarish Maharaj and his queens observed Ekadasi and Dvadasi vows for one full year on the banks of the Yamuna in Mathura. At the end of the vrata in the month of Karttik, after a three-night fast, Ambarish bathed in the Yamuna and went to Madhuvana in Vrindavan to worship Krishna. Srila Visvanath Chakravarti Thakur writes in his commentary:

"Maharaj Ambarish had observed the vow of Ekadasi throughout his life, yet he yearned to observe it for a year in the holy land of Mathura. At the end of this vrata, fasting for three nights is recommended. This means to eat simple prasad (*haviṣyānna*) once at mid-day on the Dasami and Dvadasi, and to maintain a dry fast throughout the whole of Ekadasi, day and night."

Ambarish Maharaj performed the great abhishek bathing ceremony of Krishna on a grand scale according to Vedic rituals, with *pañca-gavya, pañcāmṛta, sarvauṣadhi, mahauṣadhi,* and so on. He decorated the Lord with jewelry and fineries, and gave away silk clothes, cows, and other expensive gifts to the Brahmins. At home, he distributed to the sadhus and Brahmins millions of cows whose horns and hooves were gilded with gold and silver, and he held a grand feast for all the Brahmins.

While Ambarish Maharaj was preparing to break his fast under the directions of the self-satisfied and desireless Brahmins, the mystic Durvasa Muni arrived at his house. Ambarish respectfully received the exalted sage. He sat at the muni's feet and begged him to honor prasad at his home. The sage graciously accept-

ed the invitation saying that he had first to complete his daily ablutions and thereafter would be ready to eat. The sage went to bathe in the Yamuna and, after his rituals went into deep meditation.

Meanwhile, the auspicious moment for Ambarish to break his fast was coming to an end, but for a host to eat before a Brahmin guest is a transgression of proper etiquette. The emperor turned to his Brahmin advisors, but they were perplexed and remained silent. Ambarish decided to drink water because the Vedas have declared that *apo'śnāti tan naivāśitaṁ naivānaśitam*—drinking water can either be considered eating or not eating. The Brahmins consented to this course of action. The king then meditated on the Supreme Lord, drank a little water and waited for the sage's return.

After Durvasa Muni had completed his rituals he returned to the palace. When he saw with his mystic powers that the emperor had drunk water, Durvasa was outraged. He began to chastise Ambarish Maharaj, who stood before him with folded hands. "Look at this cruel man! Intoxicated with the pride of wealth, you think that you are God, although actually you are not even a devotee. You have transgressed the laws of religion by inviting me to dine as your guest and then eating yourself without first feeding me. Now I will show you what happens to those who commit wicked deeds like this."

Durvasa Muni tore a matted braid from his head and created a demon from it. The fearsome fire-demon held a trident in his hand and stomped around, making the entire Earth tremble, but Ambarish remained calm. Then the Supreme Lord's Sudarshan chakra, already residing with Ambarish on the Lord's order, immediately consumed the demon in flames.

Durvasa Muni was stunned by the destruction of his demon. He then saw the ominous Sudarshan rushing towards him. He ran in fear of his life, but wherever he ran the Sudarshan disc followed right behind, scalding his back with incinerating heat. Durvasa sought shelter in the caves of Mount Sumeru, in the sky, on the Earth, in the palaces of kings, and in the ocean; yet everywhere he went he felt the flaming disc bearing down on him.

He went to Brahma and Shiva begging for shelter, but they refused, knowing that he was an offender. Shiva advised him to surrender to the Supreme Lord, Vishnu. Durvasa Muni left the universe and entered Vaikuntha, the spiritual abode of Sri Narayan, and threw himself at the feet of the Lord who was relaxing with his consort Sri Lakshmi Devi, the goddess of fortune. With his body trembling and constantly feeling the heat of Sudarshan, Durvasa prayed at the Lord's feet:

"O my Supreme Lord! I have offended one of your favorite devotees. Please forgive me. If even a person living in hell becomes liberated simply by vibrating your name, then nothing is impossible for you. Please save me."

The Lord replied: "I am completely under the control of my devotees. I have no freedom. I live happily within their hearts. Even those who are devotees of my devotees are very dear to me. Without them I am nothing.

ahaṁ bhakta-parādhino
hy asvatantra iva dvija
sādhubhir grasta hṛdayo
bhaktair bhakta-jana-priyaḥ

(*Śrīmad Bhāgavatam* 9.4.63)

"O Brahmin! Just as Brahma, Rudra and the other gods are subordinate to me and were therefore unable to protect you, I too am subordinate to my devotees. I am thus unable to protect you any more than they. It is as though I were completely helpless. Those devotees who have given up all desire, even the desire for liberation, have taken over possession of my heart. I love them so much that I even hold dear those whom they protect.

"O best of the Brahmins! Without the devotees who have taken complete shelter of me, I have no desire to enjoy the eternal ecstasy inherent in my very nature, nor to take pleasure in my six supreme opulences. The devotees are the essence of my pleasure-giving potency (*hlādinī śakti*); it is they who give me joy.

"By offending Maharaj Ambarish you are ruining yourself. When one's power is used against a devotee, it harms only the one who employs it. It is the agent, not the target, who is harmed. The nature of the devotee is in no way less than mine; thus, the devotees are my only object of desire.

"How could I possibly abandon those sadhus who have given up their home, wife, children, family members, wealth, their lives and hopes for happiness in this world and the next for my sake? A faithful wife wins her husband's love by her loyalty. I have similarly been won over by my devotees who worship me with attachment while showing equanimity to all beings.

"My devotees are completely satisfied by their service to me. They do not even show interest in the four kinds of liberation that come to them as a side effect of this service, waiting for an opportunity to serve. It is thus easy to see that they would have no interest in lesser achievements like heaven!

sādhavo hṛdayaṁ mahyaṁ
sādhūnāṁ hṛdayaṁ tv aham
mad-anyat te na jānanti
nāhaṁ tebhyo' manāg api

(*Śrīmad Bhāgavatam* 9.4.68)

"I am the heart of the devotees and they are my heart. They know nothing other than me, and I known nothing other than them.

"O Brahmin! I will tell you how you can be saved from the curse that has befallen you. Go to the person whom you have offended without delay. If one curses a devotee under my protection, then that curse will return to the one who has cast it and cause him no end of grief.

"Austerity and learning are certainly good for a Brahmin, but they can be dangerous for a person who lacks humility. Spiritual power and knowledge of magic can have an effect opposite to the one intended for such a person.

"I wish the best for you, O best of the Brahmins! Therefore I tell you to go to Ambarish and pacify him for this is the only way that you can ever find peace again."

Immediately upon receiving the Lord's instructions, Durvasa Muni rushed back to Ambarish Maharaj, fell at his feet, and clasped them tightly. The emperor was extremely embarrassed at having Durvasa touch his feet, so he prayed to the Sudarshan chakra, his heart overflowing with sympathy for the sage:

"O protector of the devotees! O destroyer of all weapons, O most powerful Vaishnava, you are an expansion of the divine power. You dissipate ignorance and reveal devotion to the Lord. You terminate the jiva's warped vision of being Maya's master and give him the beautiful vision of servitorship in the form of *sambandha-jñāna*. You are the most beloved devotee of the Lord. I have forgiven Durvasa, so I beg you to now forgive him as well."

The Sudarshan chakra was pacified and saved Durvasa Muni from the pain of its scorching heat. Durvasa Muni repeatedly blessed Ambarish Maharaj saying:

"My dear king, today I have experienced the greatness of the devotees, for although I had committed an offense, you prayed for my good fortune.

"Simply by hearing the Lord's name, one is purified. So what is impossible for his devotees? You are so merciful that you overlooked my offense and saved my life. I am eternally indebted to you."

Durvasa Muni expressed his deep gratitude to Maharaj Ambarish with this and many other prayers. For the entire year over which the previous events had taken place, the emperor had been waiting for the sage's return and had not himself eaten. He now fell at Durvasa's feet in all humility and begged him to eat. After the sage had been sumptuously fed, he affectionately requested the emperor to also take prasad:

"My dear king, I am so pleased with you. At first I thought that you were just an ordinary person. Now I understand that you are an extremely exalted devotee. Therefore simply by seeing you, touching your feet, and talking to you, I feel purified and blessed. May you be glorified in heaven and on earth until the end of time."

Thus satisfied with Ambarish Maharaj, Durvasa praised him at great length before finally taking his leave. Then, by his mystic powers, he went to Brahmaloka, which is inaccessible to those philosophers who reject the true teachings of the Veda out of their attachment to dry arguments.

A full year transpired from the moment that Durvasa fled unfed from Ambarish's palace with Sudarshan chakra at his heels until the time he returned. During this entire time, Ambarish had waited patiently for his return, drinking only water — *rājāb-bhakṣo babhūva ha.* Only after Durvasa's return and after he had fed him and other Brahmins the finest rice and vegetable dishes did the great soul Ambarish himself dine. When he saw how Durvasa had been freed from the great danger and observed his own qualities of patience and tolerance, the emperor did not see these things as being a result of his own virtue, but as the doing of the Supreme Lord. In this way he remained perfectly free of pride. This is a distinguishing characteristic of the Lord's devotees.

In the days that followed, Ambarish Maharaj continued to lead a virtuous life, engaging all his senses in the service of the Lord by cleansing the temple and other activities. Always absorbed in acts of devotion to the one Absolute Truth, Vasudeva, who is manifest variously as Brahman, Paramatma, and Bhagavan, he considered even the topmost material planet of Brahmaloka with all of its opulence and pleasures to be nothing more than a royal version of hell.

At the conclusion of this story Sukadeva Goswami tells Parikshit Maharaj, "As a side effect of his single-minded devotion to the Lord, Ambarish Maharaj became free of even the faintest desire for his own sense gratification. In the end, he placed his own sons, who were as virtuous as he, on the throne and parted for the forest to end his days in service to the Lord through remembrance, or *mānasa-sevā.*

"Any person who narrates or meditates on this sublime pastime of Ambarish Maharaj will become eligible to engage in pure devotional service at Krishna's lotus feet."

The point being emphasized in this lila is that if we have committed an offense, we must submissively approach the same devotee whom we have offended and beg his forgiveness. Then the Supreme Lord, who is a slave to his devotee's love, will accept our prayers. Humbly taking the position of a servant of the Lord's servant, we will attract the mercy of the Lord. This is the ultimate gift of the pure devotees: They can give us Krishna.

In the case of Durvasa Muni, although he possessed mystic power that allowed him to physically enter Brahmaloka, Shivaloka, and even Vaikunthaloka, he still could not escape the menacing rage of Sudarshan. Though Shiva advised him to go and take shelter of Lord Vishnu himself, he found that even Vishnu was unable to protect him. We have seen in detail the reasons that the Lord felt himself unable to intervene. If we commit offenses to the Lord's devotee, we cannot find shelter at the Lord's feet. The Lord will not accept such surrender in attaining devotion to him. Though the Lord is completely independent in all respects, he gives up his independence to his devotees and becomes submissive to their will. Therefore it is said that the blessings of the Lord follow those of his devotees.

If anyone sincerely desires the mercy of the Lord, he must accept the leadership of a pure devotee; he must approach such a devotee and confide in him honestly and admit to him the misery of his existence in this world. When the devotee intervenes on this sincere soul's behalf, the Lord will hear his prayer and release him from his life of bondage. One who seeks the blessings of the Lord must learn what it means to become a servant of the servant of the Lord.

By making an example of Durvasa, the Lord taught us that we must be extremely careful not to commit offenses to his devotees. A powerful yogi like Durvasa, who was capable of going to higher planetary systems like Brahmaloka and Shivaloka, even to the abode of Lord Vishnu himself, Vaikuntha, was nevertheless unable to free himself from the dangers of Sudarshan. It was only after Durvasa followed the Lord's personal instruction and fell at Ambarish's feet, praying to him sincerely to be pardoned for his offense, that the Lord's personal weapon withdrew.

Our distorted perception of divinity cannot be rectified without the grace of Sudarshan, whose name means "real vision." The proper comprehension of the esoteric principles of Vishnu and Vaishnava eludes us without it. Proper vision means knowledge of the teachings of *sambandha*, *abhidheya* and *prayojana*. With this vision we can pierce through the darkness of ignorance by which Maya envelops us.

Accepting the sublime mood and radiance of Sri Radha, Krishna appears as Sri Chaitanya Mahaprabhu with his confidantes Ramananda Raya and Svarupa Damodar Goswami, who are the supreme teachers of the science of rasa. But the Lord himself says, "If you want to taste these divine loving sentiments, then there is no better means than chanting the Holy Names, but you will have to be more humble than a blade of grass, more tolerant than a tree, and expect no respect for yourself while offering all respects to others."

By chanting the sixteen names of the thirty-two syllable Hare Krishna Maha Mantra—without committing the ten kinds of *nāmāparādha*—one becomes eligible to enter the spiritual abode of Goloka and find the highest treasure, the prema rasa of Vrindavan. Otherwise we may chant until our tongues fall out and gain nothing. Prior to the advent of Sri Chaitanya Deva, this confidential knowledge had never been revealed. He not only revealed it, but distributed it freely. So everyone must avoid the ten kinds of *nāmāparādhas*—especially the first—to offend a Vaishnava, because a Vaishnava has taken shelter in the Holy Name and is giving his shelter to others. Violation of this principle destroys devotion.

NAMACHARYA HARI DAS THAKUR

And the Liberation of the Prostitute

SRI CHAITANYA MAHAPRABHU'S bliss multiplies without limitation when he describes the extraordinary qualities of his devotees. Hari Das Thakur, the Namacharya or supreme teacher of the Holy Name, is one such devotee. Kaviraj Goswami says, "Hari Das Thakur's greatness is immeasurable. It is impossible to describe even a small aspect of his magnanimous character."

If we try to describe Hari Das at all, it is only for our own personal purification. Vrindavan Das Thakur has also tasted the nectar of Hari Das Thakur's sublime person.

Hari Das Thakur left his home in Burhan village and traveled to Benapole, which is in West Bengal. He built a small hut in the woods and spent his time serving Tulasi Devi and chanting three hundred thousand names of God daily. Like a honeybee, he collected a little food from each righteous Brahmin home to maintain himself. The villagers were impressed with his devotion and they loved and respected him.

Ramachandra Khan was the head man of that village. Although he was born in a Brahmin family, Ramachandra Khan was a disgrace, a drunkard and a womanizer. Not only that, but he was an atheist who despised Vaishnavas. He could not bear the villagers' love for Hari Das and so he looked for a way to dishonor him in their eyes. Try as he might, however, he could find no fault in Hari Das' character.

In a final attempt to discredit Hari Das, Ramachandra Khan ordered prostitutes to be brought to him. He asked them to break Hari Das' spiritual resolve, thereby tarnishing his reputation. One beautiful young prostitute said that she required but three days to accomplish the task. Pleased, Ramachandra Khan promised to compensate her well. He commanded his guard to accompany her and, upon catching Hari Das with her in a compromised position, bring him back in chains.

The prostitute suggested that she go alone the first night and that the guard only escort her on the second. She returned home and waited for nightfall. She dressed seductively and then went to Hari Das' hut. Pretending to be devout she bowed before Hari Das and Tulasi Devi, and then sat down directly in front of him and tried to tempt him with various beguiling movements and gestures. Hari Das remained unaffected. Quite desperately, she finally made an indecent proposal to Hari Das, to which he replied, "I shall accept you without a doubt, but you will have to wait until I have finished chanting my rounds on my beads. Until then, please sit and listen to Krishna's names. As soon as I am finished, I shall fulfill your heart's desire."

Hari Das chanted continuously before the prostitute,

who remained sitting by the door. The night ended and as the eastern sky became pink with the dawn, she returned home. Later, she went and reported to Khan that she had visited Hari Das' hut and that he had promised to fulfill her wishes that night. Reassuring Khan in this way, she left for Hari Das' bhajan kutir, meditation hut. As soon as he saw her, Hari Das spoke encouragingly, "I am sorry that I disappointed you last night. Please excuse my offense. I shall certainly be with you soon. Please sit down and hear Krishna's name. As soon as my designated rounds are finished, I will attend to you and fulfill your desire."

(*Chaitanya Charitāmṛta Antya* 3.120-121)

The prostitute could not fathom the real meaning of Hari Das' words because her consciousness had been clouded by lust. However, a distinct change was already visible in her. That night, she offered obeisances to Tulasi Devi and sat down by Hari Das' door listening to his soft chanting. Soon she also began to chant, "Hari...Hari...Hari." Once again, night ended and it was dawn. She became restless and Hari Das said, "I have vowed to chant ten million names this month and this vow is now nearing its end. I thought that I would complete it today, but I am still not finished in spite of having chanted through the whole night. However, I am sure that tomorrow I will finish and my goal will be reached. Then it will be possible for me to enjoy you in full freedom."

The prostitute returned to Khan that morning and again informed him of what had happened on the previous night, keeping his hopes alive. That evening, she went to Hari Das' cottage for a third time. After offering obeisances to Tulasi and Hari Das, she sat on the threshold where she could listen to Hari Das' incessant chanting, and she also began to chant the holy name of the Lord, "Hari, Hari, Hari." Hari Das compassionately told her, "Today I will complete my vow ; then I will satisfy all your desires."

The good fortune to associate with a great soul for three nights and to hear the pure name from his lips can never go in vain. The third night passed with Hari Das' continuous chanting of the Holy Name. But with the coming of the third dawn, a new awakening also took place in the heart of the young prostitute. The gloom of ignorance shrouding her consciousness lifted and a fire like the blazing sun burnt up all of the impurities in her heart.

She fell to the ground at Hari Das' feet. Weeping, she pleaded for her sins to be forgiven. She confessed that Khan had employed her to seduce him and said, "Because I am a prostitute I have performed many sinful acts. Dear master, please be merciful to me. Deliver my fallen soul."

Hari Das replied, "I know everything about Khan's conspiracy against me. He is an ignorant fool, but that doesn't bother me. I would have left this place the day Khan began plotting against me, but I stayed here for three days just for your sake, to benefit you."

The prostitute said, "Please be my guru. Tell me what I should do to get relief from material existence."

Srila Hari Das replied, "Go home and immediately distribute all your possessions to the Brahmins, Then return here and live in this cottage. Always chant the Holy Name of Krishna and serve Tulasi by watering her daily and offering her prayers. Do this and you will quickly find shelter at Sri Krishna's lotus feet."

Hari Das Thakur left the village after initiating the

prostitute with *kṛṣṇa-nāma*. Understanding that the guru's instruction must be executed without hesitation, she gave away all of her belongings. She gave up her home, shaved her head, and lived in her guru's bhajan kutir. She eagerly engaged in devotional practices, chanting day and night three hundred thousand Holy Names, serving Tulasi Devi, eating frugally, and observing the various fast days.

Śrī Chaitanya Charitāmṛta says, "She gradually subdued her senses and the symptoms of divine love manifested in her. She became a celebrated devotee and many Vaishnavas came to visit her. Everyone was astonished to see the sublime transformation in her character. They glorified the potency of Hari Das and offered him obeisances."

By receiving a Vaishnava's blessings, even a prostitute can become a pure and advanced devotee. On the other hand, Ramachandra Khan, even though a Brahmin by birth, had to undergo severe suffering because of his malicious behavior to Hari Das Thakur. Ramachandra was a non-Vaishnava by nature, but he compounded this fault by offending a great devotee like Hari Das. This made him a demon or asura, for criticizing and blaspheming the devotees is the principal characteristic of the demonic class of men.

Srila Bhaktisiddhanta Saraswati Prabhupada writes in his *Anubhāṣya*: "Ravana, the son of Vishrava, hated the Supreme Lord, and for this offense he was called an asura or demon, even though he had been born in a Brahmin family. Similarly, Ramachandra Khan also became known as an asura because of his offenses to a great devotee."

The results of Ramachandra Khan's offenses took terrifying shape in his life. It so happened that the Lord Nityananda Prabhu was traveling all over Bengal with a large group of disciples and associates, intent on propagating the Holy Name and subduing atheistic forces. One day he happened by Ramachandra Khan's house and sat down in the Chandi mandap, a covered area consecrated to the goddess Durga. Wealthy non-Vaishnava families built separate areas to worship the goddess Durga and this area was used for entertaining guests when not being used for puja.

Lord Nityananda's large party filled up the entire courtyard. Ramachandra Khan should have been filled with gratitude at the immense good fortune of having his house sanctified by the touch of Nityananda Prabhu's lotus feet. As a host, he should have personally come out to welcome Nityananda Prabhu, but he sent one of his servants instead, thereby insulting him and his exalted followers. In a curt message to the Lord, the servant informed him that since he was with a large group that could not be properly accommodated, arrangements had been made for all of them to go elsewhere.

Sri Nityananda Prabhu

What followed is described in the *Chaitanya Charitāmṛta*: "When Nityananda Prabhu heard this order from Ramachandra Khan's servant, he became very angry and came out of the mandap laughing madly and said, 'Ramachandra Khan is right. This place is only suitable for cow-killing meat-eaters. It is quite unfit for me.'"

To show his displeasure with Khan's behavior,

Nityananda Prabhu stormed out of his house and left the village. The unfortunate Khan was so foolish that he ordered his servants to dig up the earth where the Lord had sat, and then had it filled up again after it had been cleansed with water and cow dung. Even the courtyard where the Lord's followers had been sitting was cleansed in this way, as though they had contaminated his grounds by their presence. Even then, Khan felt as though he had not done enough.

Sri Krishna and His eternal friends

It was not long before the consequences of offending the Supreme Lord and the Vaishnavas took effect. It so happened that Khan had been cheating the government by tax-evasion. Enraged by Khan's dishonesty, the Muslim finance minister stormed into his house one day and camped on his Durga mandap. He ordered that a cow be slaughtered and its flesh cooked on that very spot. For three days Khan's family was bound and held captive while the minister's men pillaged his household and the entire village. On the fourth day, the magistrate and his men left the village, its properties destroyed and everyone shocked and in agony. Khan was completely ruined and forsaken.

Kaviraj Goswami concludes: "Everyone living in a place where an advanced devotee has been disrespected must suffer the consequences, even if the fault lies with only one person amongst them."

In spite of hearing about or even experiencing the fatal consequences of offending the Supreme Lord or his devotees, we are so deluded that we still need to be reminded not to commit offenses.

After leaving Benapole, Hari Das went to Chandapura, where he stayed as a guest in the house of one Balaram Acharya. Chandapura was one of the villages that made up the town of Saptagram, now called Triveni. It lay to the east of the home of Hiranya and Govardhan Majumdar, two brothers who were the local treasurers of government tax revenues. Balaram and Yadunandana Acharya were priests to the Majumdar family.

Balaram Acharya was a very devout Brahmin and a great devotee who had been favored by Hari Das' grace. He took care of all Hari Das' needs while the saint spent his days chanting three hundred thousand Holy Names in a hut.

At this time, Govardhan, Majumdar's son, who was later known as Raghunath Das Goswami, was just a schoolboy. Raghunath regularly visited and associated with Hari Das, who showered his blessings upon him. As a result of these blessings, Raghunath Das later came to the lotus feet of Sri Chaitanya Mahaprabhu.

Raghunath Das Goswami is a *nitya-siddha*, or an eternal confidante of Sri Chaitanya Mahaprabhu who descended into this world as part of Mahaprabhu's entourage. His association with Hari Das is meant to exemplify that bhakti is only attainable by the mercy of an exalted devotee of the Lord.

One day, Balaram Acharya respectfully invited Hari Das to attend a religious assembly at the Majumdar residence along with many pandits and respectable gentry. When Hari Das arrived with Balaram Acharya, Hiranya and Govardhan received him with respect. The scholars present there also generously expressed their appreciation of him, giving great pleasure to the Majumdar brothers, who were no mean scholars themselves.

The pandits particularly praised Hari Das for his vow to chant the Holy Name three hundred thousand times every day. This started a discussion of the glories of the Holy Name. Someone in the assembly said that chanting the Holy Name absolves the chanter of all sins. Another observed that the Holy Name bestows liberation. Hearing people speaking of only the external effects of *kṛṣṇa-nāma*, Hari Das pointed out that these were not the principal results of pure Nāma:

"What you say is not the true result of *kṛṣṇa-nāma*. Its real effect is to awaken ecstatic love of Krishna. Even the Lord loves his own name."

Hari Das then quoted a verse from the *Bhagavatam* to support his contention:

evaṁvrataḥ sva-priya-nāma-kīrtyā
jātānurāgo druta-citta uccaiḥ
hasaty atho roditi rauti gāyaty
unmādavan nṛtyati loka-bāhyaḥ

"As one continues his vow to chant, the Lord becomes more dear to him, and so does his Holy Name. With increased enthusiasm, he becomes deeply attached to Krishna and he loves the name of Krishna so much that he sometimes laughs out loud, sometimes cries in separation, or even exhibits loving anger. Sometimes the ecstasy is so intense that he sings and dances like a complete madman, not caring for anyone or anything."
(*Śrīmad Bhāgavatam* 11.2.40)

Visvanath Chakravarti says that *evaṁ-vrataḥ* means that the vow to chant *kṛṣṇa-nāma* regardless of circumstances gives prema bhakti yoga, union in devotional love. The person who upholds such a vow is beyond any of the concerns of this world. He states further that among the nine limbs of devotion, Nāma kirtan, or chanting the Holy Name, is the highest. *Sva-priya-nāma-kīrtyā*—"Krishna's name is very dear to Krishna" —this Sanskrit phrase refers to any person who through chanting Krishna's name has fallen in love with him. At this stage the heart has become like gold due to the heat from the fire of yearning to see Krishna.

Why does the devotee laugh? Visvanath gives the example of a devotee meditating on the Lord's Vraja lila: As Krishna the butter-thief slips into a gopi's house early in the morning, an older gopi sitting near the door warns the other gopis that Yashoda's son has snuck into the storeroom. She cries, "Catch him! Catch him!" As he sees this pastime in his mind's eye, the devotee laughs in joy at the sight of Krishna running away to escape from the gopis.

The next moment, when the devotee awakens from this vision, he laments: "Oh no! The unlimited ocean of bliss was within my reach and now I have lost him!" He cries pathetically in separation from Krishna, even screaming, "Where are you? Talk to me!"

When Krishna hears such a devotee's plea, he reassures him: "Here I am—I came running to you as soon as I heard you call." Then the vision is regained and the devotee resumes praising the Lord. Dancing madly, he shouts, "I am so happy, today my life is perfect." At this stage, the devotee couldn't care less about praise or criticism. This condition is described by the following verse from Rupa Goswami's *Padyāvalī* (73):

parivadatu jano yathā tathā vā
nanu mukharo na vayaṁ vicārayāmaḥ
hari-rasa-madirā-madātimattā
bhuvi viluṭhāma naṭāma nirviśāma

"Drunk on the wine of rasa we become like madmen rolling on the ground, and sometimes dancing wildly. People may think that we are crazy, but who cares?"

Such an awakening of Krishna prema is the natural and direct result of *kṛṣṇa-nāma* — not merely the destruction of sin or achieving liberation. Hari Das cited the example of a sunrise. The result of sunrise is light; the dissipation of darkness is secondary. He quoted a verse from the *Nāma-kaumudī* of Sri Lakshmidhara Swami and asked the scholars to explain it. But they preferred to have Hari Das enlighten them.

aṁhaḥ saṁharad akhilaṁ
sakṛd udayād eva sakala-lokasya
taraṇir iva timira-jaladhiṁ
jayati jagan-maṅ galaṁ harer nāma

"All glories to that holy name of the Lord, which is auspicious for the entire world. As the rising sun immediately dissipates all the world's darkness, which is as wide as an ocean, so the holy name of the Lord, if chanted once without offenses, can dissipate all of our sins."

Hari Das explained, "Just before sunrise, before the sun is even visible, it eliminates the darkness of night. With the first glimpse of sunlight, all fears vanish; and when the sun is actually visible, everything is revealed and a new day begins. Similarly, with the first hint of *kṛṣṇa-nāma*, the reactions of sinful life are instantly terminated. And when one chants the Holy Name offenselessly, ecstatic love of Krishna is awakened. Although liberation is readily offered by Krishna, it is nothing to a pure devotee. In the *Śrīmad Bhāgavatam* it is stated, 'While dying, Ajamila unintentionally chanted the Holy Name of the Lord by calling for his son Narayan and he entered the spiritual world. What, then, can be said of those who chant the Holy Name with deep faith?'"

Krishna says, "My real devotees want nothing from me. They don't want to live where I live, have the same wealth I have, nor have a body like mine — they just want to serve me."

One of the Brahmins present was Gopal Chakravarti. He was the chief tax-collector and official messenger of the Muslim ruler. He could not stand Hari Das' explanation that even a shadow of the Holy Name could give liberation. He spoke with anger and scorn:

"You are all supposed to be pandits and you sit here listening to this fool rave about *kṛṣṇa-nāma*. Do you really believe that liberation, which one who is in complete, absolute knowledge of Brahman cannot attain even after millions of births, can be attained by a devotee through the mere reflection of the Holy Name?"

Hari Das replied, "Why do you doubt it?" The scriptures say the joy of knowledge of Brahman is like a puddle when compared to the ocean of happiness that comes from tasting the Holy Name:

tvat-sākṣāt-karaṇāhlāda-
viśuddhābdhi-sthitasya me

sukhāni goṣpadāyante
brāhmāṇy api jagad-guro

"My dear Lord, you are so beautiful that I feel like I am drowning in an ocean of nectar just looking at you. Whatever other concepts I had of happiness are now like puddles of mud." (*Hari-bhakti-sudhodaya* 14.36)

The Brahmin said: "If you believe that one can be liberated by the mere shadow of Krishna's name, then prove it by cutting your nose off."

Hari Das replied: "If it is not so, then I most certainly will cut off my nose."

Everyone was shocked to hear Gopal Chakravarti's impudence. The Majumdars were outraged and began to chastise him. Balaram Acharya also reprimanded him: "You are just caught up in absurd rhetoric; what do you know about the process of devotion? Yet you have the audacity to insult Hari Das Thakur? You're committing spiritual suicide!"

Balaram Acharya called Gopal a *ghaṭa-paṭiyā* pandit, a scholar who is addicted to useless arguments. He was hinting that Gopal Chakravarti had read a little of the Indian philosophy of logic, or Nyaya, and now thought himself to be a great debater. Unfortunately, he had become so proud of his puny knowledge that he dared insult a great devotee of the Lord. The Majumdars ostracized Gopal from the assembly not only for his offense to Hari Das, but because he minimized the glories of the Holy Name, which he considered to be exaggeration.

Hari Das himself rose to leave the assembly, but everyone fell at his feet, begging forgiveness. Hari Das never saw the faults of others and smiled compassionately at them, saying: "None of you are at fault. Even this ignorant Brahmin is not at fault because he is accustomed to dry speculation and logic. One cannot understand the glories of the Holy Name simply by logic and argument. Therefore that man cannot possibly fathom the glories of the Holy Name. Do not be sorry because I was insulted. Return to your homes, and may Krishna bless you."

The reactions for committing aparadh did not take long to manifest. Within three days the Brahmin was infected with leprosy, and as a result his nose melted and fell off. His toes, limbs, and fingers, which were as delicate as flower buds, withered into stumps. The people were astonished to see this phenomenon, and they were in awe of Hari Das' spiritual potency and offered obeisances to him.

"My real devotees want nothing from Me. They don't want to live where I live, have the same wealth I have, nor have a body like Mine. They just want to serve Me."

Krishna Das Kaviraj notes, "Although Hari Das did not take the Brahmin's offense seriously, the Supreme Personality of Godhead did, and the Brahmin suffered the consequences. A characteristic of a pure devotee is that he excuses the offenses of the ignorant, but Krishna never tolerates an offense to the lotus feet of his devotee."

When Hari Das learned about Gopal contracting leprosy, he was deeply sorrowful. He left Balaram Acharya's house and traveled to Sri Advaita Acharya's home in Shantipur. Hari Das prostrated himself before the Acharya, and Advaita picked him up and embraced him lovingly. Sri Advaita built a hut for Hari Das on the bank of the Ganga and arranged for him to conduct his meditation and worship there.

Hari Das continued his daily routine of *kṛṣṇa-nāma*, honoring prasad at Advaita's home and hearing Krishna katha. Together they dove deep into an ocean of bliss discussing Krishna and Mahaprabhu.

Sri Gauranga Mahaprabhu

MAHADEVA SHIVA

And Sati's Sacrifice

VISHNU, THE Supreme Godhead, is known as Yajnesvara, the lord of sacrifice. The *Śrīmad Bhāgavatam* tells the story of how he nevertheless refused to grace King Daksha's sacrifice because Daksha had insulted the topmost Vaishnava Shiva by not inviting him there. The Lord holds his devotees so dear that he cannot abide those who insult them. Govinda does not accept the worship of one who tries to please him while making no effort to please his devotees. He considers such a puffed up servant to be an arrogant pretender and finds no pleasure in his service.

Daksha's daughter and Shiva's devoted wife Sati could not refuse Daksha's invitation because he was her father, so she attended despite her husband's disapproval.

At the assembly, her father began to publicly malign Shiva. Sati was deeply pained and thought, "Feeling sentimental, I ignored my husband's warning and came to my father's house only to be tormented by hearing blasphemy against an elevated Vaishnava. Shame on me a thousand times! I don't know what to do. I cannot continue to live in this wretched body of mine, which was conceived by my blasphemous father. I will abandon it and purify my soul by bathing it in the dust of my godly husband's feet."

She then addressed her father Daksha, "My Lord Shiva is dear to all living beings; he loves everyone and has no enemies. Who else but you could behave in such a despicable manner to such a godly personality?

"A saintly person's nature is to overlook other's faults and only appreciate their good qualities. But an envious person like you sees even the good qualities of others as faults. The *madhyama-adhikārī* Vaishnava properly discriminates between good qualities and bad qualities. The *uttama-adhikārī* discovers everyone's smallest good qualities and praises them as if they are traits of greatness, whereas a fool decries a great personality who possesses all divine qualities."

The nature of fault-finders is to only look for other's faults. They disregard the many good characteristics in others and attempt to portray them as shortcomings. Ants will search for little holes and cracks even in a beautiful gem-studded temple. Such people are like sieves that conveniently overlook their own thousand perforations but ridicule a pinhole and try to magnify it.

A saintly person is free from fault-finding. The *Chaitanya Charitāmṛta* defines a first-class Vaishnava in the following way:

uttama hañā vaiṣṇava habe nirabhimāna
jībe sammāna dibe jāni' kṛṣṇa adhiṣṭhāna

"Although a Vaishnava is the most exalted person, he is prideless and respects everyone, knowing that Krishna dwells within them."
(*Chaitanya Charitāmṛta, Antya* 20.25)

Sati continued, "Anyone who limits his concept of the self to the body, mind, or intellect is deluded. It is not surprising that such fools malign exalted persons. However, elevated souls calmly tolerate all blasphemies hurled against them. They are undisturbed by praise or criticism, honor or dishonor, though their followers, who are like particles of pollen clinging to their lotus feet, never tolerate blasphemy. They want to destroy the offenders.

"The two syllables forming the name 'Shiva' — *śi* and *va* — are so auspicious that even uttering them unintentionally removes all inauspiciousness and evil. Shiva's instruction is law, his pastimes are most holy and glorious, and he is the best friend of all living beings. Therefore, only an envious fool could even think of criticizing him."

Daksha responded, "You have described the sublime characteristics of saints and warned against finding faults in others, but what about me? I am a Brahmin and what is more, one of the Prajapatis (progenitors). Everyone honors me. You are my daughter and therefore you of all people should respect me. Do you not think it is an offense to criticize me?"

Sati replied, "How can you, an enemy of Shiva, speak of blasphemy? As a party to this heinous offense I should kill you, and by not doing so I am worsening my own offense."

Then she recited the following verse:

karṇau pidhāya nirayād yad akalpa īśe
dharmāvitary aśṛṇibhir nṛbhir asyamāne
chindyāt prasahya ruśatīṁ asatīṁ prabhuś cej
jihvām asūn api tato visṛjet sa dharmaḥ

"Upon hearing blasphemy of Lord Shiva, the protector of religion, devotees should plug their ears and go away if they are unable to punish the blasphemer. But if they are not in a position to enforce corporal punishment, then it is their duty to give up their own life."
(*Śrīmad Bhāgavatam* 4.4.17)

In his commentary to this sloka, Srila Visvanath Chakravarti writes:

"In the ancient times of India, the *kṣatriya-dharma*, or rights and responsibilities of the military class, allowed that a Kshatriya was empowered to punish blasphemers. The other classes of Vedic society — Brahmin, Vaishya and Shudra — were not permitted to mete out physical punishments. Thus, Vaishyas (merchants) and Shudras (workers) may give up their lives as a reaction to hearing blasphemy. It is not right for a Brahmin to give up his life, so he should cover his ears, chant the name of Vishnu, and leave the company of the blasphemer, feeling deeply saddened." Since Vaishnavas are at least equal to the Brahmins, they are to follow the Brahmin code.

Srila Jiva Goswami writes in his *Bhakti-sandarbha*, in the context of *sādhu-nindā*, the first of *nāmāparādhas*, that it is damaging even to overhear blasphemy of a Vaishnava. He quotes the *Bhāgavatam*:

nindāṁ bhagavataḥ śṛṇvaṁs
tat-parasya janasya vā
tato nāpaiti yaḥ so'pi
yāty adhaḥ sukṛtāc cyutaḥ

"Upon hearing blasphemy against the Supreme Lord or his devotee, any person who does not leave that unholy place is implicated in the offense and loses all *sukṛti*, spiritual merit."
(*Śrīmad Bhāgavatam* 10.74.40)

Sri Jiva comments, "The instruction to leave the place of offense is solely directed at those who are weak. Those who are strong and powerful must retaliate. Those incapable of either of these courses of action should give up their lives."

Srila Bhaktisiddhanta Saraswati Thakur Prabhupada writes in his purport of the *Śrīmad Bhāgavatam* 4.4.17:

"The Brahmins are the gurus of the entire Varnashram society. The Brahmin's guru is the Vaishnava acharya, or the spiritual preceptor and protector of Vaishnava theology. At the first sign of blasphemy against an acharya, it is one's duty to leave. However, if one is not in an appropriate position to enforce corporal punishment, he should give up his body, feeling unbearable distress and shame.

"Those on the mental platform are opposed to Vishnu and the Vaishnavas. They see everything in the temporal and destructive light of this opposition. They thus naturally have differences of opinion. Though they may be damaged as a result of the conflicts arising from their commitment to the mental platform, the divine reality is never affected. No good can come out of their sectarian debates, however. Scriptures therefore repeatedly tell us to avoid the company of those who are inimical to the path of devotion. Both the scriptures and the saints ordain renunciation of the company of the impious. Bhaktivinoda Thakur therefore sings:

vaiṣṇava caritra sarvadā pavitra
jei ninde hiṁsā kari
bhakativinoda nā sambhāṣe tāre
thāke sadā mauna dhari

Mahadeva Shiva in Meditation

"The Vaishnava's character is always pure. Bhaktivinoda will never speak to envious people who criticize such a Vaishnava, and vows to always remain silent in their company." (*Kalyāṇa-kalpa-taru*)

Srila Bhaktisiddhanta Prabhupada also says that one should not only strictly avoid the association of the Vaishnava aparadhi, but also the company of the aparadhi's friends.

Sati, the exalted wife of the greatest Vaishnava, Lord Shiva, continued to berate her father fearlessly: "I can't stand living in this rotten body born from your seed. If one mistakenly drinks poison, doctors recommend vomiting. My poisoned body needs to be rejected and burned. You are so vile that I am ashamed to be your daughter. My husband addresses me as *Dākṣāyaṇī*, 'the daughter of Daksha.' When I think of that and how this name binds me to you, I feel disgusted and my heart breaks. I want to kill myself."

After finishing this emotional criticism of her father, Sati suddenly went into a deep meditation and, by her mystic power, left her body. Shocked, everyone began to wail. Daksha remained silent and Sati's bodyguards, the Pramathas and Guhyakas, rose up to kill him. Seeing them advance, the powerful sage Bhrigu chanted a potent mantra from the *Yajur Veda* and offered oblations into the sacrificial fire. Thousands of powerful heavenly warriors known as Ribhus, armed with magical weapons, arose out of the fire and began to rain blows on Sati's bodyguards. Outnumbered by these superior warriors, Sati's guards fled in all directions.

Meanwhile, Narada Muni, who had been observing

the entire incident with his mystic vision, went to Lord Shiva and told him everything. In a fit of rage, Lord Shiva tore a lock of matted hair from his head and dashed it to the ground. The hair transformed into an expansion of Lord Shiva, the monstrous warrior named Virabhadra, who bowed in deep reverence to his master and prayed for instructions. Shiva said, "You are the embodiment of my anger. Now go and lead my forces in the destruction of Daksha and his sacrifice!"

Virabhadra immediately put Shiva's order into action, overrunning Daksha's sacrifice along with the Pramathas and Guhyakas. Virabhadra himself arrested Daksha, while another of Shiva's servants, Maniman, captured Bhrigu; Chandesvara caught Surya while Nandisvara tied up Bhagadeva. The sacrificial priests and attendants were horrified by the turn of events and fled wherever they could, but Shiva's army rained stones down on them, killing or wounding them all.

Bhrigu Muni had been about to offer an oblation into the fire when Virabhadra tore his mustache from his face as a punishment for having twirled it while derisively laughing at Lord Shiva. Virabhadra slammed Bhagadeva to the ground and ripped his eyes out because he had encouraged Daksha by winking at him while he was insulting Lord Shiva. And because Pusha had smiled, baring his teeth while Shiva was being abused, Virabhadra knocked his teeth out, just as Balaram did to Dantavakra.

Then Virabhadra sat on Daksha's chest and attempted to severe his head with a sharpened sword. At first he was not capable of doing so and was quite astonished to see that he was unable to pierce even the skin of Daksha's neck. Finally, Virabhadra found a special axe in the sacrificial arena, meant for beheading animals to be used in the sacrifice. With this, he was able to cut off Daksha's head, which he threw into the sacrificial fire as an oblation.

Virabhadra then set the whole arena on fire. Having completed the desecration of Daksha's yajna, he called for Shiva's soldiers and left for Kailasa. Any sacrificial ceremony in which there is blasphemy of a pure Vaishnava will face the same destruction.

In their omniscience, Brahma and Narayan had stayed away from Daksha's sacrifice, knowing beforehand what would be the terrible outcome. The demigods, progenitors and sages, who had tolerated Daksha's insults to Shiva without objecting, had been rebuked and chastised as they fled the arena. Severely wounded and fearing for their lives, they approached Brahma with pleas for protection. Brahma listened patiently as they narrated the gory episode to him and then advised them:

"Those who vilify a powerful personality and then desire to live in peace will find their desires filled with inauspicious consequences. You have offended Shiva, who is a recipient god of the sacrificial oblations. You must be sincerely remorseful and throw yourselves at his feet. He is called Ashutosh, which means 'very easy to satisfy,' so try to please him. When he is angry he is capable of destroying the entire universe. He has been deeply hurt and enraged by the death of his beloved consort. I see no recourse other than sincerely begging forgiveness at his lotus feet."

Brahma then led Indra and the other gods to Lord Shiva's abode, Kailasa. They found him sitting under a tree and meditating on the Supreme. They offered Shiva their respectful obeisances and he reciprocated. Brahma prayed and begged him to excuse Daksha and to find a way for him to complete the yajna. He further pleaded with him to forgive the other gods who had been a party to the heinous crime and were now suffering the results of their actions, and to heal the maimed and wounded guests so that everyone could receive their share in the sacrifice.

Brahma and the gods appeased Shiva who then placed a goat's head on Daksha and brought him back to life by his mystic power. The others who had been wounded in the battle were also healed. Shiva accompanied them to Daksha's sacrificial arena, where Daksha fell at his feet and begged for mercy. The yajna resumed and this time Narayan came to receive oblations; Shiva and Brahma were worshiped and received the

The Wedding of Shiva & Parvati

remnants of the sacrificial offerings—Daksha's yajna was completed. In time, Sati reincarnated as Parvati, the daughter of Menaka and Himalaya, and married Shiva again.

By hearing this sacred tale of Shiva, who is the crest jewel among Vaishnavas, we advance on the path of devotion.

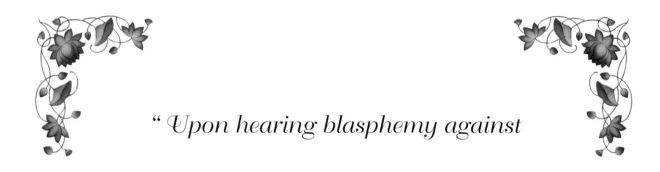

"Upon hearing blasphemy against the Supreme Lord or his devotee, any person who does not leave that unholy place is implicated in the offense and loses all sukriti, spiritual merit."

Srimad-Bhagavatam

Sri Narada Muni

And the Sons of Daksha

In Christian Theology there are the Ten Commandments; in Vaishnavism there are the ten offenses against the Holy Name. To blaspheme one who has taken complete shelter of the Holy Name and who shelters others in *kṛṣṇa-nāma* is so serious that it is listed first and foremost of the ten. A devotee must be extremely cautious, otherwise he could commit spiritual suicide. An offender may chant the Holy Name for millions of lifetimes without receiving the blessings of Nāma Prabhu, the Holy Name himself.

The scriptures inform us that Daksha was beheaded because he offended Shiva. After he pleased Shiva with sincere remorse, he was forgiven, yet Vaishnava aparadh is so insidious that if even a trace of it remains in the heart, there will be remission. Daksha, who committed Vaishnava aparadh in the time of the Svayambhuva Manvantara, had to suffer its consequences eons later. As the *Śrīmad Bhāgavatam* states:

"Following the order of the creator Brahma to procreate, all the Prachetas accepted Marisha as their wife. From her womb Daksha took another birth. Daksha had to take birth again due to his offenses to Mahadeva Shiva."

Srila Visvanath Chakravartipada gives his opinion: "In Svayambhuva Manu's era, Sri Narayan gave birth to Brahma from the divine lotus that sprouts from his navel. Daksha was Brahma's son, yet even so, because of offending Mahadeva Shiva, he had to suffer taking birth again from the womb of Marisha. Consequently Daksha had to die twice: first at the hands of Virabhadra and a second time of natural causes."

The material universe is destroyed at the end of the fifth manvantara. Daksha was born in the Svayambhuva Manvantara. Desiring immense opulence, he performed austerities for a period of five manvantaras. During the sixth manvantara, the Chakshusha, he became very rich. Visvanath Chakravarti states that it was by the mercy of Shiva that Daksha acquired his fabulous wealth.

In the Chakshusha Manvantara, on the orders of the Supreme Lord Hari, the progenitor Daksha accepted Asikni as his wife and fathered ten thousand sons, who as a group were known as Haryashvas. Daksha instructed his sons to increase the population. In order to prepare themselves spiritually for their task as progenitors, he told them to visit the holy lake of Sri Narayan Sarovar near the mouth of the Indus River, where many saints had lived since the beginning of time. By the purifying influence of the water of the lake, Daksha's sons were freed of material desires and they wished to take up the renounced order of life, the path to becoming paramahamsas.

Nevertheless, the Haryashvas remembered their father's instruction to populate the world and began to undergo a process of self-purification. The great sage Narada found them performing their penances and examined them by asking them ten esoteric questions. Understanding the import of these questions, they became detached and decided to pursue a life of devotion. They expressed their appreciation to Narada and gave up their promise to return to family life.

When Daksha heard that his sons had become renunciates he was overcome with lamentation: "Alas! Even good sons can be the cause of great sorrow!" This is the power of Vishnu's Maya, for under her influence fathers and mothers are often heard to complain in this way.

Brahma managed to console Daksha, who then fathered another thousand sons, the Saralashvas. Daksha gave them the same instruction he had given to their elder brothers — to get married and have many children, to populate the earth. Following in the footsteps of the Haryashvas, the Saralashvas traveled to the same holy place where their brothers had attained spiritual perfection. As soon as they touched the waters of the Narayan Sarovar, their hearts were cleansed of all material contamination. For the next few months they performed austerities, first drinking only water and then fasting completely. All the while they worshiped the Supreme Lord Vishnu by chanting the following powerful mantra,

oṁ namo nārāyaṇāya
puruṣāya mahātmane
viśuddha-sattva-dhiṣṇyāya
mahā-haṁsāya dhīmahi

"Obeisances to Narayan, the supreme person and the supreme soul, always fixed in his abode of pure goodness. We meditate on him, the great swan."

(*Śrīmad Bhāgavatam* 6.5.28)

While they were engaged in these austerities, Narada again happened by. Once again, he asked them the same riddles he had asked the Haryashvas. He furthermore encouraged them to follow the example of their elder brothers. He said,

"My dear Saralashvas, sons of Daksha! Listen to my counsel, which I give you for your own benefit. You should follow the path taken by your brothers, the Haryashvas, for it is the way to achieve the greatest good."

Narada is the embodiment of devotion to Vishnu. Once he had blessed the young men and departed, it was not long before they also became committed to the auspicious life of asceticism.

Meanwhile, Daksha's anxiety was increasing with several inauspicious omens. When the news reached him that his younger sons had also taken up the path of renunciation and disappeared, Daksha was again overwhelmed with grief. Once more Narada Muni was the cause, and when he happened upon Narada, Daksha cursed him, his lips trembling with anger. "You wear the dress of a saintly person, but you are not actually a saint. On the other hand, though I may be a family man, I am a real saint. By convincing my sons to renounce family life, you have done me a great injustice, though I had never wronged you."

It is said that at birth, a Brahmin is indebted to the rishis, the gods and goddesses, and to his father.

Shiva, Parvati & Ganesh on their carrier Nandi

According to the scriptures, a Brahmin can be cleared from his debts to the rishis by observing brahmacharya (celibacy) until marriage, to the gods by performing yajnas, and to his father by producing sons. Daksha argued that his sons had not yet absolved their debts and were therefore not eligible for renunciation. Daksha felt that Narada's instruction had made his sons apathetic to family life, which disqualified them from receiving benediction in this life and the next. Further, Daksha felt that Narada had confused their immature minds. He told Narada that his association with the Supreme Lord was a blemish on the Lord's reputation. Daksha said,

"You have no compassion and you are shameless. You represent Vishnu and boast that you are his associate. Actually, you are giving him a bad name. It doesn't seem right that someone who ruins Vishnu's reputation should be considered his devotee and friend.

"You act with enmity towards those who have never done you any wrong, disrupting their loving relations with their friends and family members. We have heard that the Lord's devotees act out of compassion for all beings. It seems that you are unworthy to be a devotee.

"If by vibrating the Holy Name of Krishna our hairs do not stand on end, our eyes do not flood with tears, and there is not a volcanic eruption of ecstasy in our bodies, our hearts must be covered in steel."

"So you are just a devotee by virtue of your dress and not by behavior. Do you think that simply taking up the path of asceticism one can be freed from the attachments of the householder life? Real renunciation comes about as a result of real knowledge and experience and not simply as a result of fancy words. All you have done is disturb their intelligence.

"Without experiencing fully the life of the senses, no one can understand their illusory and ultimately painful nature. This can only come about as a result of experience. When this happens, then one naturally becomes disinterested in the sensual life. The same result cannot come about as a result of instructions alone, no matter how beautifully argued.

"We are engaged on the path of works, living a saintly family life according to the Vedic injunctions. But by disrupting our religious principles you have behaved in a way that is completely intolerable.

"We could tolerate your actions the first time. You made me lose my sons once, but now you have done it again. You do not know how to treat people properly. So though you may continue to travel all over the universe, I curse you to never have a home anywhere."

Narada, who is respected by all saintly persons, responded to Daksha's curse without protest, saying, "So be it." If one accepts a curse and allows it to take effect, even though he is capable of counteracting it, then such tolerance should be enough to win over the person who cursed him. The truth is that for those who are mired in materialism, Daksha's viewpoint has value, whereas Narada's teachings on pure devotion are outside their grasp. And this leads to Vaishnava aparadh.

Verily the famous saying is true that "the tendency to a life of engagement is natural to all, but renunciation leads to the greatest reward (*pravṛttir eṣā bhūtānāṁ nivṛttis tu mahāphalā*)."

Meanwhile Daksha, lamenting the loss of his sons, was consoled by Brahma. He was encouraged by Brahma to try to have children again, but this time he was afraid that if he had sons again, the same thing would happen. So he fathered sixty daughters who were very devoted to their father. They all married — ten daughters were given to Dharma, thirteen to the sage Kashyapa, twenty-seven to the moon-god Chandra, and the rest to other sages — and their children and grandchildren populated the universe.

Nevertheless, the purpose of this story was to show the far-reaching effects of offenses to the Vaishnavas. In the Svayambhuva Manvantara, when Daksha offended Lord Shiva, he asked forgiveness, but did so half-heartedly. The disease of aparadh remained in Daksha's heart and resurfaced as an offense to the lotus feet of Sri Narada Muni, even after he had taken another birth in the sixth manvantara. This is to be expected. Even if one worships the Lord for millions of lifetimes, if he has offended a Vaishnava it will be impossible to gain the Lord's mercy. This is a warning to all devotees: If ever one finds oneself in a position of committing an offense to Vaishnavas, then he should apologize sincerely, otherwise he can count on its having far-reaching effects.

" Krishna lila is the cream of all nectar,

only the confidantes of Sri Radha and Krishna

and the eternally perfect souls can enter there.

So how then should we conceive of Chaitanya lila?

The pastimes of Sri Chaitanya Mahaprabhu

are an infinite reservoir, from which thousands

of streams of the nectar of Krishna lila are flowing

in all directions, inundating everyone everywhere.

May the swan of my mind swim there eternally,

and dive deep into its infinite waves of nectar."

SRI GARUDA

The Divine Carrier of Vishnu

EVEN A GREAT YOGI becomes lusty and falls down if he offends a pure devotee. The consequences of offending an elevated Vaishnava are extremely grave.

During the time of Krishna's incarnation, in the land of Vrindavan, there was a rather large lake in the Yamuna River. Because the river current did not flow through it, the lake's water was practically stagnant. Worse still, a poisonous snake Kaliya had made his home there, killing all the fish and making the water undrinkable. The lake became known as Kaliya's Lake or Kaliyadaha. How Kaliya came to take up residence in the Yamuna is a long story that is also instructive in our understanding of Vaishnava aparadh.

In ancient times, the island of Ramanaka, which was one of the nine *varṣas* that make up Jambudvipa, was the home of the snakes. It was the custom of human beings to go to Ramanaka Island every month to leave some offering to the snakes in order to appease them and thus escape being bitten and poisoned. The snakes in their turn were much afraid of Garuda and so they would leave a portion of these offerings for him on the full moon and new moon days.

Amongst the snakes, Kaliya was particularly proud of his powerful poison and so began stealing the offerings meant for Garuda and eating them himself. Garuda, who is an exalted soul and renders Vishnu direct service as his personal conveyance, was angered by this impudence and came to challenge Kaliya. The two began to fight and though Kaliya tried to bite Garuda with his poisonous fangs, the great eagle was able to beat him with his wings. So much so, that Kaliya was forced to flee for his life and take shelter in the lake that came to bear his name, knowing that Garuda would not be able to follow him there.

The reason that Garuda was unable to go there was the result of other events. Long before Kaliya had contaminated the lake in the Yamuna, a yogi named Saubhari Rishi lived there for many years and practiced severe austerities, sometimes levitating above the surface of the water and sometimes meditating deeply submerged within it.

One day Garuda was passing by the Yamuna. Being hungry, he dived into the lake even though Saubhari prohibited him from doing so. Garuda swooped down and plucked a large fish that he thought would be ideal for his lunch. The smaller fish were frightened upon seeing their leader so easily consumed. Saubhari Rishi felt sorry for them and cursed Vishnu's winged carrier: "If you dare to ever come here again, you will die!"

The great commentator on the *Śrīmad Bhāgavatam*, Visvanath Chakravarti Thakur, explains the offensive nature of this curse: "Unfortunately Saubhari Rishi committed two offenses against the great devotee Garuda: giving orders to a superior personality (*ājñā-pradāna*), and exhibiting a malicious attitude (*tad-iṣṭa-prātikūlya*). Garuda, on the other hand, could not be faulted for disobeying Saubhari's order (*ājñā-laṅghana*) or for his violence to other beings (*prāṇi-hiṁsana*), because of his exalted position.

"Saubhari committed a third offense by cursing a parshad, an associate of the Lord. He did this to protect the helpless creatures living in the lake, but his compassion was in vain because subsequently Kaliya's venom poisoned those waters and all the fish died anyway. So, in a futile attempt to show mercy to the fish, Saubhari brought the terrible consequences of aparadh upon himself. It is said that the road to hell is paved with good intentions."

Saubhari's curse was literally that if Garuda ever came to the lake to eat fish, he would immediately die. The implication, however, was that he would perish, even if he simply came there without eating fish. As a result, Garuda never ventured near the lake. Kaliya knew about this curse and so took shelter there when he needed to escape Garuda.

While Saubhari Rishi was performing his austerities, the great king Maharaj Yuvanashva, the ancestor of Ambarish Maharaj, was trying to produce an heir. He tried every possible means to conceive a child through his hundred wives, but remained unsuccessful. Totally dejected, he entered the forest with his wives. The compassionate sages of the forest initiated a sacrifice to satisfy Indra so that he would bless the king with a son.

The sages performed the sacrifice with great care and prepared a potion that was to be drunk by the king's principal queens in order to fertilize them. After finishing the ritual, they left this potion in a chalice within the sacrificial arena. During the night, the king awoke from his sleep feeling thirsty, found the chalice and drank its contents. The next morning the sages discovered the empty chalice and were alarmed. When they learned that the king had drunk the water, they understood that this could only have happened by God's intervention. They offered prayers to the Lord, accepting his divine act, and said, "Fate is all-powerful. Man is helpless before destiny."

In time, an exquisite son with all the marks of a powerful prince appeared from the lower right side of King Yuvanashva's abdomen. The baby cried continuously, clamoring for breast-milk, and the sages were confused about how to feed it. Just then Lord Indra, who was being worshiped in the yajna, appeared and comforted the crying child. He offered the baby his index finger to suck, saying *māṁ dhātā* — "You may drink me." Thus the prince became known as Mandhata.

Although the baby was born from the abdomen of King Yuvanashva, the king did not die due to the blessings of Indra and the sages. He remained in that spot and performed severe austerities, finally achieving yogic perfection.

The baby grew up and eventually became emperor. He drew strength from Vishnu and ruled the seven islands that comprise the Earth — Jambu, Plaksha, Shalmali, Kusha, Krauncha, Shaka, and Pushkara. Powerful demons like Ravana were always fearful of him, and hence Indra called him "Trasaddasyu," one who scares rogues away. It used to be said that the sun always shone on Mandhata's kingdom.

Emperor Mandhata gave immense wealth in charity and performed yajnas to worship Vishnu. He fathered three sons and fifty daughters through his wife Bindumati, the daughter of Shashabindu. The sons were Purukutsa, Ambarish, and the great mystic Muchukunda.

Meanwhile, the time had arrived for Saubhari Muni's

offense to Garuda to ripen and bear fruit. One day, the sight of a pair of fish mating diverted his attention and his heart filled with lust. Impelled by desire, he came up from the riverbed and went to Mathura where he approached Emperor Mandhata and requested the hand of one of his daughters in marriage. The emperor replied that he could marry whichever one of his daughters would have him. After all, it was time for their *svayaṁvara*, a ceremony in which princesses themselves chose a husband.

Saubhari Rishi thought to himself: "I am old, wrinkled and gray because of my austerities, so I am not attractive to young women. In a way, the king has refused me by leaving it up to a princess to choose me. I must make myself so handsome that even the heavenly damsels will dream of having me as their husband." So, by his mystic power he transformed himself into a handsome young man.

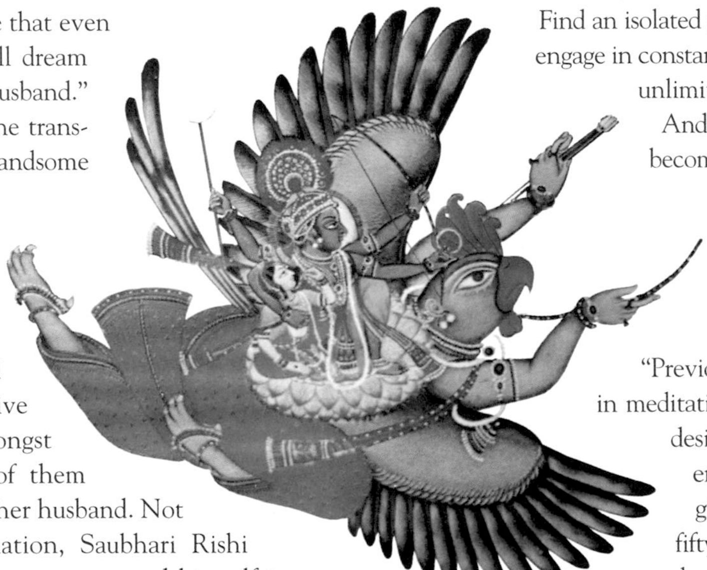

When the royal guards escorted Saubhari into the women's quarters, all fifty princesses found him so irresistibly attractive that they quarreled amongst themselves, every one of them wanting to have him for her husband. Not intimidated by the situation, Saubhari Rishi again used his mystic powers to expand himself into fifty forms so that he could marry them all. After the wedding, he built fifty magnificent palaces so full of splendor that the palace of Lord Indra himself paled by comparison. Despite his own huge empire, Mandhata was awestruck and humbled by Saubhari Rishi's opulence and royal lifestyle.

Although Saubhari was surrounded by fantastic luxury and enjoyment, he did not feel satisfied or at peace with himself. Just as butter fuels fire, sense gratification increases a man's lusty desires. Saubhari's desire for enjoying the life of the senses continued to grow until one day he finally became apathetic to these enjoyments. Full of remorse for the time he had wasted in sensual pursuits, he gave the following warning to the people of the world:

"Just look at how I have destroyed myself. Because of the offense I committed to Garuda while performing penances in Kaliya's lake, I became attracted to sex life simply by looking at fish! As a result, all of my spiritual power has been lost. Learn from my experience and be careful.

"Anyone who is interested in finding liberation should avoid the company of people who devote their lives to the erotic arts. Do not waste your time dwelling on external sense objects. Find an isolated place where you can engage in constant meditation on the unlimited Supreme Lord. And if at any time you become lonely, associate with saints who have taken complete shelter at the Lord's lotus feet.

"Previously I was absorbed in meditation on Hari, but sex desire dragged me into endless family entanglements. I married fifty wives and fathered a hundred sons through each of them. So we became 50,000 in number. Material nature corrupted my conscience to such an extent that I considered the pursuit of sense objects to be the ultimate goal of life. But there is no end to desires for enjoyment in this world or the next."

Saubhari Rishi passed his days in lamentation. He finally tried to detach himself from his family entanglement by retiring and entering the forest, followed by his devoted wives. Once again he began to practice austerities and at the time of his death he offered himself totally in the service of the all-pervading Supersoul. His wives also attained the same spiritual

Kaliya Naga, his devoted wives & Sri Krishna

goal because of their devotion to him.

In the Tenth Canto of the *Śrīmad Bhāgavatam*, Krishna's glorious pastimes of chastising the Kaliya serpent have been described. There we learn that Krishna once went to the Yamuna with all his cowherd boyfriends, with the exception of Balaram. Balaram was kept at home by his mother Rohini and Yashoda because it was his birthday and he had to take a special bath and perform some religious rituals. But whenever Balaram was absent from the work of grazing the cattle, it seemed that something unusual always happened to Krishna. That was true on this day also.

Some of the calves ran ahead and were followed by a number of young cowherds, while Krishna came leisurely up the rear. By the time the calves and boys reached the river, the sun was high and they were feeling very hot and thirsty. So thirsty, in fact, that they drank the contaminated water of the Kaliyadaha. In a few moments, the boys and the calves were lying lifeless on the riverbank.

Krishna's compassion for his beloved friends is infinite and with his ambrosial glance, he revived them. Of course, their deaths were only appearance, for these eternal associates of the Lord are free from the fetters of death. Krishna's Yogamaya occasionally creates such situations in order to create interesting situations for the pleasure of the Lord and his devotees.

When they had recovered, they looked at Krishna in amazement and said, "We were dead and now we are living again. How did that happen? Did someone say a spell or give us some medicine to revive us?" After a while, they concluded that it was their comrade Govinda who had looked on them with his transcendental compassion.

It was apparent that the problem of the poisoned lake

needed resolution, so Krishna climbed up the only living tree on the bank and jumped into the water and began joyfully swimming in the lake. Kaliya considered himself to be the undisputed ruler of the lake and he was angry that his realm had been invaded. He attacked Krishna by coiling himself around his body and trying to bury his fangs into it.

It is significant that there was only one living tree on the banks of the Kaliyadaha. Different reasons have been given for this tree's resistance to Kaliya's poison. Some say that it was given the strength to survive in the hope of getting the touch of Krishna's feet in the future. In other Puranas, however, it is said that Garuda had once perched in its branches with a jug of the heavenly ambrosia known as *amṛta*.

Krishna's companions and the calves were paralyzed at the sight of their friend motionless in the great serpent's coils. In the meantime, various ominous signs were troubling the denizens of the cowherd village. Krishna's parents thought, "Balaram did not go with the boys today, so something terrible must have happened."

They and the rest of the Vrajavasis followed Krishna's footprints up to the lake and, trembling with apprehension, saw the frightening battle taking place in the stagnant waters. Some of them were prepared to risk certain death by jumping in after Krishna in an attempt to save him from Kaliya's clutches, but Balaram stopped them, as he knew of Krishna's superhuman powers. He assured them that Krishna was perfectly capable of taking care of himself.

Indeed, when Krishna saw the anxiety of his friends and family, he freed himself from the many-headed serpent's grasp, jumped onto one of its hoods and began dancing. As the original master of dance and the musical arts, Krishna put on a performance that attracted all the musicians and terpsichoreans of Svarga. The Siddhas, Charanas, Gandharvas and Apsaras all watched enraptured from their heavenly seat and provided musical accompaniment or showered flowers on the Lord, while other demigods sang the Lord's glories.

Kaliya had never bowed his thousand heads before anyone, but now the repeated pounding of Krishna's dancing feet forced him to bend them forward. It is Krishna's nature to destroy the pride of the arrogant and Kaliya was a witness to his power to do so. Blood began to flow from his nose and mouth. He began to vomit and his entire body went slack. Soon he began to understand that the person dancing on his head was the origin of all being and he surrendered to him.

Kaliya's numerous wives and their children were quite pious, unlike their husband. Seeing their husband at the threshold of death, they came to appeal to the Lord for his liberation. Folding their hands in prayer, they glorified the Lord,

"Lord, you have appeared in this world to chastise the wicked, therefore it is only just that you punish our husband. You are equal to all, so when you punish your enemy, it is to show mercy to him and all his entourage. We can deduce that our husband was a great sinner in previous lives, for how else could he have taken birth as a venomous serpent. But whatever sins he may have committed, you have destroyed them with the blessed touch of your feet. We also consider your anger to be a blessing to us, who are so poor and powerless.

"Perhaps our husband did something uncommonly pious in one of his previous lives that made him deserving of such a blessing. Perhaps he was once humble and respectful, or perhaps he engaged in some rigorous penance, or acted altruistically in the interests of the unfortunate. How else could you have been so pleased with him?

"The goddess of fortune, Lakshmi, gave up all pleasures to take shelter of this land and perform extensive austerities, all in the hope of getting a few grains of dust from your feet. Yet she was unsuccessful. We cannot fathom why she failed while our sinful, toxic husband was able to receive that dust in great quantities on his heads. We can only surmise that no amount of penances or austerities can earn your mercy. Your blessings can have no material cause. You did more than simply touch his heads with your feet; you danced on them like a madman. What divine bliss he must have experienced while you danced! A million lifetimes of pious activities could not have earned him even a fraction of that bliss.

"O Lord! Please treat our husband as a son and a dependent. He could not help his actions due to the terrible circumstances of his birth as a serpent. He did not know your glories and offended you and those dear to you. Please forgive him. The terrible force of your steps has brought him to the threshold of death. Please think of us helpless women and give us back our life by reviving him. Please tell us what to do so that we may become your servants and remain free from the bondage of our deeds."

The prayers of Kaliya's devoted wives moved the Lord and he descended from the great serpent's head. Kaliya's physical and moral strength slowly returned and he himself started to address some prayers to Krishna.

"O Lord! This universe is your creation and we snakes are your creatures. We have taken birth in this species and so by nature we are given to envy, anger and ignorance. Every creature is afflicted by the dispositions of its kind and such things are not easily thrown off. We are under the control of your illusory energy. How can any of us overcome this all-encompassing power? It is therefore up to you to decide whether to punish or to forgive us."

The Lord, enjoying his pastimes in human form, answered, "You cannot stay here, so return to the ocean, to the island of snakes whence you came. Let the cattle and people of my village use the waters of the river without fear. Those who remember how I have chased you away from here will never fear snakes again."

Srila Visvanath Chakravarti Thakur says that these two verses can be recited like a spell to protect one from snakes. In his *Sārārtha-darśinī*, he also quotes a relevant mantra said to be from the *Ṛgveda*,

yamunā-hrade hi so yāto yo nārāyaṇa-vāhanaḥ
yadi kālika-dantasya yadi kākālikād bhayam,
janma-bhūmi-paritrāto virviṣo yāti kālikaḥ

"Garuda, Lord Narayan's mount, came to visit the lake in the Yamuna. If there is any fear of Kaliya's fangs or if there is any fear of his poison, then it is gone. The Lord who protects his land has made Kaliya harmless."

Krishna continued, "Whoever bathes in this spot and offers oblations to the gods with its waters or who fasts and worships me, will be freed of all sins. O Kaliya, you fled Ramanaka Island from fear of Garuda and took shelter in this lake. From now on, if Garuda ever sees you, he will leave you alone because of the mark of my foot on your head."

Then Kaliya and his wives worshipped the wonderful Lord. Indeed the pastimes of the Lord are wonderful. He saved the Vrajavasis from the danger presented by Kaliya and then he delivered Kaliya from the fear of Garuda. Indeed, the Lord delivered Kaliya from offenses he had committed to both his devotee Garuda and the residents of Vraja, but it was ultimately due to the faith and devotion of the pure-hearted wives of the snake. The black serpent was aware of this and he prayed to the Lord as follows:

"O Lord! You have shown the highest degree of compassion because I am the lowest of the low. No one is a greater sinner than I and no one is more merciful than you. You have given me a gift that has never been given to anyone else in the universe – you have imprinted my forehead with the auspicious marks of your feet.

"I offensively attempted to poison you by biting your delicate body with my great fangs. Now I wish to cool your wounds with these gifts of sandalwood and musk and dress you in these clothes and garlands."

After Kaliya and his wives had worshipped the Lord in an appropriate fashion, they took the Lord's permission to depart for the island of the snakes in the middle of the ocean. As soon as he left, the waters of the Yamuna returned to their original, crystal-clear purity.

One of the gifts Kaliya's wives gave the Lord was the Kaustubha jewel. In the *Gaṇoddeśa-dīpikā*, it is said that this gem is one of the Lord's eternal symbols and is always with him. However, when he appeared in human form in this world, the jewel disappeared and somehow found its way into Kaliya's storehouses. As they were giving their treasures to the Lord as tokens of their gratitude, they also gave him the Kaustubha.

Kaliya and his wives pleased the Lord with their sincere worship and so the Lord also touched him with his lotus hand, blessing him with fearlessness, ridding him of all his pain. Once again, Kaliya spoke, saying, "Lord, on whose flag flies the image of Garuda! Today I consider myself to be the servant of Garuda's older brother. I would also like to be able to serve you by acting as your vehicle. If ever you need to travel to a distant place, even a hundred thousand miles away, I will take you there in the blink of an eye." Indeed in some Puranas it is said that Krishna rode to Mathura on Kaliya's back when he was ordered to go there by Kamsa.

This incident gives insight into the subtle workings of Vaishnava aparadh. The powerful sage Saubhari committed an offense at the feet of Garuda in an act of sympathy to a fish. Because of his actions, he not only indirectly orchestrated the mass extinction of every living creature in the Yamuna River, but was also the cause of harassing the exalted residents of Vrindavan (Vrajavasis) by creating a haven for Kaliya. Thus Saubhari offended even the Vrajavasis, who are the most dear to Krishna.

Saubhari had wanted to show his compassion for the fish there, but in the long run, he caused them to be wiped out by the poisonous presence of Kaliya. His compassion for the fish led him furthermore to harshly condemn the irreproachable Garuda, the dear servant of Lord Vishnu. His anger at the sacred eagle and his act of cursing him led to spiritual disaster. He gave up the pleasures he knew from meditating on Brahman. He exchanged his years of penance for a youthful body so that he could purchase the love of the princesses and enjoy the hellish pleasure of mundane sex life. Only after a lengthy time of such entanglement did Saubhari finally grow indifferent to his life of regal sensuality by virtue of his long association with Krishna's abode.

But as far as relishing the nectar of Krishna bhakti was concerned, he could not obtain it. Kaliya, on the other hand, although envious and capricious, was aided by the good wishes of his devoted wives, who attracted the mercy of Krishna and brought him all auspiciousness.

It is almost impossible to be released from the consequences of Vaishnava aparadh. Without feeling deep remorse and without surrendering at the feet of the offended devotee, one can never be forgiven. Without such forgiveness, the goal of life is lost.

Srivasa Pandit

And the Liberation of the Leper

WHILE ON HIS WAY TO MATHURA accompanied by large numbers of associates, Mahaprabhu stopped in the village of Ramakeli for a few days. Then, instead of continuing on to Mathura, he turned back south and started on his return journey to Jagannath Puri. On the way, he stopped at Sri Advaita Acharya's home in Shantipur. There a leper came to visit Mahaprabhu. The leper threw himself before the Lord, crying for mercy.

"My Lord! You are supremely compassionate. You have appeared in this world to save the most unfortunate souls. Your heart is naturally pained to see people suffer. I am a leper. Please tell me how to get free from my excruciating pain."

Mahaprabhu screamed: "Get out of my sight! Just by looking at you my body is defiled. Even someone who is very pious will have to suffer if he sees you. You have blasphemed a Vaishnava; no one is more sinful than you. If you cannot endure the suffering you are experiencing now, I don't know how you will endure what happens to you after death, when you go to the worst of hells.

"You have insulted Srivasa, a Vaishnava whose very name sanctifies the universe. Even Brahma and the gods sing his glories. By worshipping him one attains Krishna's lotus feet, which are inaccessible to even Shiva or Ananta Sesh. There is nothing greater than to serve him. He is to Krishna than Ananta Sesh, Lakshmi, Brahma, more dear to Shiva, and even the Lord himself.

"In the *Śrīmad Bhāgavatam*, Krishna says to his beloved friend Uddhava: 'Even though Brahma is my son, Shiva is my other self, Sankarshan is my brother, and Lakshmi is my wife, they are not as dear to me as you are.'

"Anyone who blasphemes such a Vaishnava suffers untold misery, birth after birth. The offender's learning, high birth, and religion are useless. All his worship is refused by Krishna. Mother Earth is purified by the touch of a Vaishnava like Srivasa. He purifies all directions just by his glance. When he dances with his arms upraised, even the heavens are freed from any residues of anxiety.

"Srivasa Pandit is a *mahā-bhāgavata*, yet you criticized his spotless character. Therefore your body is in burning pain from leprosy, but this punishment is nothing compared to what Yamaraj has in store for you. I hate having to even look at you. Even I cannot deliver you."

Sri Chaitanya Deva's words shocked the leper, who fell down praying:

"I must have been mad to blaspheme a Vaishnava. I

didn't realize the seriousness of my actions. Now I am suffering, as indeed I should. You are God and I know that you desire my welfare. Furthermore, it is the nature of sadhus to relieve the suffering of others. They are compassionate even to offenders. So I beg you to give me shelter. If you abandon me, then who else will come to my rescue? You know all the remedies and penances for the different offenses, so as the omnipotent universal father, please tell me what penances I must perform. I accept that my suffering is a just punishment for my actions."

Mahaprabhu said: "Being afflicted with leprosy certainly seems to be a terrible punishment, but it pales in comparison with the torments that will follow you life after life. Yamaraj has sixty-four hells that await those who are guilty of such offenses.

"You have offended Srivasa Pandit, so it is from him that you must beg forgiveness. Go fall at his feet. Only if he excuses you can you be absolved of your offense. A thorn in the body is removed from the same cut it makes when entering. A thorn stuck in the foot can't come out of the shoulder. Similarly, one must approach the Vaishnava he has offended and plead forgiveness. Only if the Vaishnava agrees will he be forgiven. Here, I have given you the means by which you can be released from your suffering.

"Srivasa Pandit's heart is absolutely pure; fall at his feet and beg for shelter. He never sees faults in others and will forgive you. You will be liberated and your misery will disappear."

All the devotees began to cheer. The leper bowed to Mahaprabhu in appreciation of his unlimited mercy and left in search of Srivasa Pandit. When he found Srivasa, he threw himself at his feet and begged forgiveness. That magnanimous and compassionate crest-jewel among Vaishnavas, Srivasa Thakur, then pardoned the leper and he was liberated.

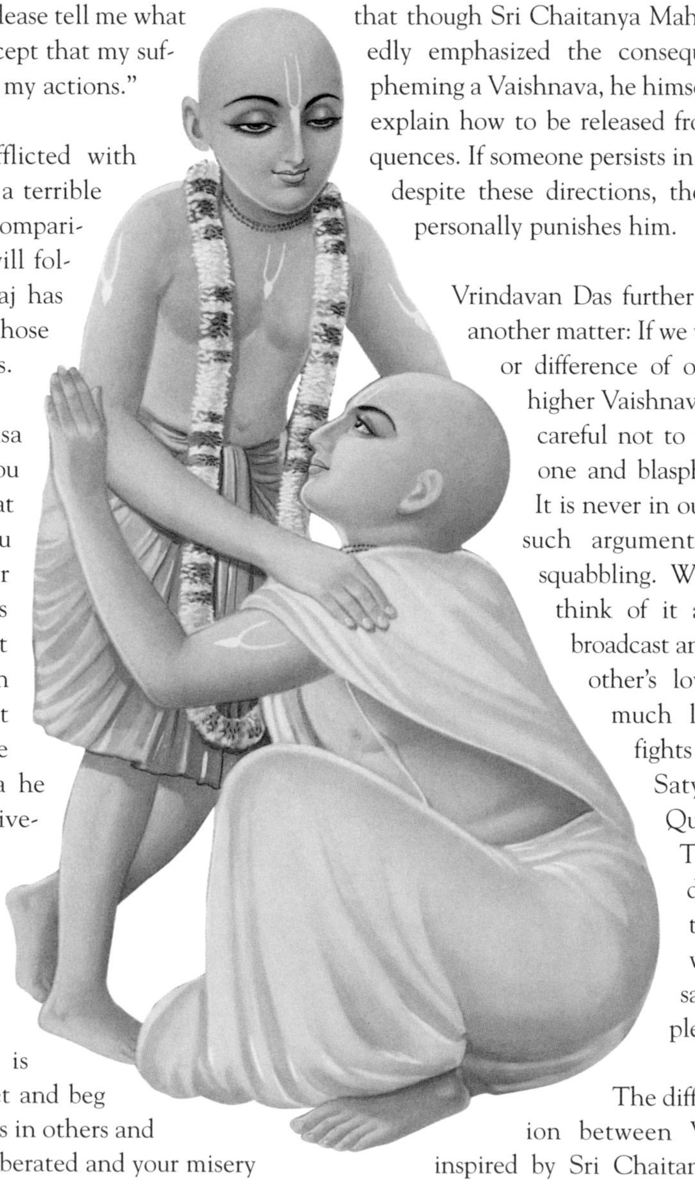

Vrindavan Das warns us in the *Chaitanya Bhāgavata* that though Sri Chaitanya Mahaprabhu repeatedly emphasized the consequences of blaspheming a Vaishnava, he himself was careful to explain how to be released from these consequences. If someone persists in such blasphemy despite these directions, then Mahaprabhu personally punishes him.

Vrindavan Das further warns us about another matter: If we witness a quarrel or difference of opinion between higher Vaishnavas, we should be careful not to take the side of one and blaspheme the other. It is never in our interest to see such arguments as mundane squabbling. We should rather think of it as a vehicle to broadcast and enhance each other's love for Krishna, much like the verbal fights between Queen Satyabhama and Queen Rukmini. The transcendental subject of their arguments was always the same — how to please Krishna.

The differences of opinion between Vaishnavas are inspired by Sri Chaitanya in order to instruct us. If anyone foolishly takes sides in such a debate, he becomes an aparadhi by contradicting and criticizing the other Vaishnava, and the results are most harmful to him. It's like someone serving Krishna with one hand and slapping him with the other. When we understand that Vaishnavas are the different limbs of Krishna's transcendental body, we understand that the Lord and his devotees are inseparable.

> *"Even Brahma and the gods sing the glories of Srivasa. By worshipping him one attains Krishna's lotus feet, which are inaccessible to even Shiva or Ananta Sesh. There is nothing greater than to serve him. He is more dear to Krishna than Ananta Sesh, Lakshmi, Brahma, and Shiva; he is even more dear to the Lord than the Lord is to himself."*

If we worship Krishna and his devotees as one, and remain immersed in serving Krishna's lotus feet, then we will become immortal. Any person who sincerely narrates or hears these auspicious instructions will always be protected from committing Vaishnava aparadh.

The point to consider here is that sometimes the dissension between pure Vaishnavas gives pleasure to Krishna because they are fighting over him. But if a devotee is infected by *nāmāparādha* and is driven to offend a humble Vaishnava, then no sympathy can be extended to him.

There are numerous instances in the scriptures that describe such self-destruction. The *Hari-bhakti-vilāsa* cites a sloka from the *Skanda-purāṇa* that was spoken by Markandeya Rishi to Bhagiratha:

"Those rascals who criticize a Vaishnava not only fall down to a hellish destination, but drag their forefathers with them. There are six sources of fall down in our dealings with Vaishnavas: physically harming them, blaspheming them, feeling hatred for them, not extending the proper etiquette to them, showing anger to them and not feeling joy upon seeing them."

It is well known that the Vaishnava should avoid bad association. The critic of the Vaishnavas is the worst association. The *Śrīmad Bhāgavatam* says:

tato duḥsaṅgam utsṛjya
satsu sajjeta buddhimān
santa evāsya chindanti
mano-vyāsaṅgam uktibhiḥ

"Persons with developed consciousness and high intellect must completely reject bad association and seek the company of saints, because their instructions alone can free us from the mental attachments that drag us down."

Srila Bhaktivinoda Thakur says that even a guru who blasphemes Vaishnavas must be rejected. "At first one may be a qualified guru, but if for some reason he becomes an offender to the Holy Name, he gradually begins to lose his power of discrimination. He then blasphemes a Vaishnava and loses his taste for *kṛṣṇa-nāma*. Gradually he sinks into the clutches of materialism and the exploitation of women."

Narottama Das Thakur & Srinivasa Acharya

Srila Visvanath Chakravarti Thakur explains the word *vyāsaṅgam* in the above verse to mean the "attachments that drag one down." Srila Sanatan Goswami states in his *Dig-darśinī* commentary on the same verse in *Hari-bhakti-vilāsa*:

"The term *satsu* refers exclusively to the devotees of the Supreme Lord and not to fruitive workers, philosophers, or yogis. Bad association (*duḥsaṅgam*) means excessive attachment to family, friends, and home. It also means relationships motivated by exploitation. Only the wisdom of saints can save us from our tendency to exploit and lead us on the path of spiritual service."

Sri Ganesh

Book Bhagavata & Bhakta Bhagavata

The Education of Devananda Pandit

MOST LIVING BEINGS ARE OVERWHELMED by selfish desires. This selfishness leads to their being bombarded by the blows of material nature. They are easily blinded by anger and frustration and lose all understanding of what is important and what is not. They make no effort to control their thoughts or speech. They thus say whatever comes into their minds about the Vaishnavas and the spiritual master, even allowing feelings of hatred to fester against them. Such feelings may eventually lead to overt inimical action.

It is quite normal for ignorant, conditioned souls under the influence of the illusory energy to think themselves wise and learned. In fact, however, they lead lives that are twisted and unethical, abandoning the one way that leads to the ultimate good. The consequence of such ignorance is that they suffer the pangs of old age, disease and death and remain on the merry-go-round of repeated births in heaven and hell.

If such people present themselves as spiritual leaders, however, they become sanctimonious hypocrites who do unlimited damage to others. As stated in the *Kaṭha Upaniṣad,* one blind person cannot show another blind person the way — both will fall into the ditch. Similarly, one who pretends to have wisdom will only cause the same tragic consequences to happen to his blind followers.

No one was more vocal in condemning Vaishnava aparadh than Vrindavan Das Thakur. He quotes the *Nāradīya-purāṇa* to say, "One who is openly fallen hurts only himself, whereas a phony saint is worse, because he drags all of his followers down with him."

Pretenders usurp the elevated seats of saints and misguide the general populace in the name of religion. They encourage the public to engage in false practices and to criticize the actual representatives of religious principles, the Vaishnavas. They destroy themselves as well as their unfortunate followers. Unwary people gather to hear spiritual instructions from these charlatans, but end up hearing insults against actual saintly persons. Believing in such teachings, followers of false gurus pave their path to hell.

Vrindavan Das says: "People eagerly come to hear spiritual instructions from someone they think is saintly based on his external appearance. Unfortunately, instead of receiving nectar, they may hear criticism directed against real saints and so plunge deep into the abyss."

Vrindavan Das tells of a situation like this that arose in the time of Lord Chaitanya.

A certain scholar named Devananda Pandit lived in Vidyanagar, a village on the western bank of the Ganges across from Nabadwip where Sarvabhauma

Sri Chaitanya's intimate associates

Bhattacharya's father, Mahesvara Visharad, also made his home. Devananda had earned a reputation as a teacher of the *Bhāgavata-purāṇa*. The public held him in high esteem not only for his learning but also for the strictness of his renunciation, for he maintained a life of asceticism as rigorous as that of a sannyasi.

Unfortunately, due to a strong desire for liberation and a lack of devotion, he could not comprehend the real import of the *Bhāgavatam*, which is an ocean of liquid love, bhakti rasa. He possessed jnana, but due to aparadh had not realized that Krishna is the ultimate goal. Mahaprabhu's secretary Svarupa Damodar indicated that if someone wants to truly understand *Śrīmad Bhāgavatam*, he must hear it from a Vaishnava after completely taking shelter of the lotus feet of Sri Chaitanya Mahaprabhu.

Devananda was a learned Brahmin, a life-long celibate who led an austere life and so Vrindavan Das said that he had some of the qualifications needed to understand the meaning of the *Bhāgavatam*. However, he had not been able to do so due to his offensive behavior towards genuine Vaishnavas. Indeed, despite his numerous good qualities, because of his neglect of the path of pure devotion, he committed a grave aparadh at the feet of an exalted pure devotee of the Lord.

Srila Prabhupada comments: "Every living entity is by nature a Vaishnava. As such, Devananda Pandit had the potential to know the imports of the *Śrīmad Bhāgavatam*, but since his eternal nature as the servant of Krishna was dormant, his insight was impeded because of aparadh. For that reason, his qualification to understand was immediately removed. Krishna knows everything and he alone could recognize that Devananda had an offensive mentality despite his engagement in the study and preaching of the

Bhāgavata. Ordinary people did not possess the far-reaching vision to recognize this defect in Devananda."

One day, Mahaprabhu was walking through Vidyanagar with his associates. He arrived at a dike by a rice paddy near the house of Sarvabhauma Bhattacharya's father, Mahesvara Visharad. Devananda Pandit had built his dwelling by the side of this embankment. Mahaprabhu was passing by just as Devananda was delivering a lecture on the *Bhāgavatam*. Mahaprabhu overheard part of his commentary, but what he heard did not please him, for bhakti yoga played no part in it. Mahaprabhu became enraged and spoke out:

"How dare this rascal interpret the *Bhāgavatam*? He is completely ignorant of its essence. On what authority does he speak? The *Bhāgavatam* is the literary incarnation of Krishna and devotion to Krishna is described in it as the ultimate goal of human life.

"The four Vedas say that the *Bhāgavatam* is a manifestation of divine love. The Vedas are like cream that Sukadeva Goswami churned to produce the *Bhāgavatam*, its butter-like essence, which he then served to Pariksit Maharaj. Sukadeva is very dear to me and he is fully conversant with the esoteric truths revealed in the *Bhāgavatam*. The *Bhāgavatam* is full of descriptions of my absolute position and nature, all of which are approved by me. Whoever makes the slightest distinction between me, my pure devotees and the *Bhāgavatam* is doomed."

Although the Lord spoke these words in anger, the Vaishnavas were greatly pleased with the instructions. He continued:

"Anyone who does not recite the teachings of the *Bhāgavatam* in the light of bhakti is wallowing in ignorance. This rascal is continuously talking without a single mention of bhakti; I will shred his copy of the book!" The Lord stepped forward, but the Vaishnavas pleaded with him not to carry out his threat.

The *Śrīmad Bhāgavatam* is eulogized throughout the Vedas as the most profound and esoteric work of literature. Poisoned by education and pride, a so-called pandit cannot grasp this truth. One who boasts of fully comprehending the *Bhāgavatam* completely misses its essence. One who knows that it is nondifferent from the inconceivable Supreme Lord is enlightened about its purport — pure devotion.

Devananda Pandit was resplendent with all good qualities. Rarely does one meet a personality of such high stature. However, those who have a false understanding of the *Bhāgavatam*, as well as those who praise them, are punished by Yamaraj, the universal judge.

Srila Prabhupada expands on the last of these statements:

"In spite of being a highly talented and cultivated scholar, one may not understand the essence of the *Bhāgavatam*. Those who attempt to glorify such scholars are subject to the chastisements of Yamaraj, who assesses our deeds and rewards or punishes us accordingly." (*Gauḍīya-bhāṣya* to *Chaitanya Bhāgavata, Madhya* 21.27)

"If you want to understand Srimad Bhagavatam, you must hear from a real Vaishnava."

In other words, if a learned scholar like Devananda Pandit could misunderstand the purport of the *Bhāgavatam*, then how much more difficult it will be for fools like us who merely pose as scholars of that transcendental literature? We will have to face the consequences of our hubris when we meet Yamaraj on the Day of Judgment.

Mahaprabhu's anger toward Devananda Pandit was rooted in an event that had taken place before Mahaprabhu's appearance, when the Earth was devoid of devotional ecstasy. Devananda had committed offenses against Srivasa Thakur, the incarnation of Narada Muni, the personification of devotion. At that time there were only a small number of devotees scattered here and there, and they were suffering on account of the world's indifference to love of God. The scholars of Nabadwip were engaged in studying the *Gītā*, *Bhāgavatam* and other scriptures, but unfortunately none of them were teaching their true meaning, Krishna bhakti. Since these pandits never cultivated a service attitude, they were unable to appreciate the devotional conclusions of these literatures.

One day the great devotee Srivasa Thakur wanted to hear a discussion on the *Bhāgavatam*, so he came to Devananda Pandit's lecture and sat in the audience. The entire *Śrīmad Bhāgavatam* is composed of transcendental syllables steeped in devotional relish of love of Godhead. Upon hearing the *Bhāgavatam* slokas, Srivasa Thakur entered a deep state of ecstasy. The eight manifestations of deep spiritual emotion (*aṣṭa-sāttvika-vikāra*) such as shivering, hairs standing on end and weeping overwhelmed him. He started to let out long sighs and then to cry. The audience, which consisted mostly of students who had a purely empirical view of the world, felt disturbed by these transformations, as they interfered with their listening to the Pandit's discourse. The students dragged Srivasa Thakur, who was completely oblivious to them, and placed him outside. Devananda Pandit raised no objection to this act of malice. Gradually, when Srivasa Thakur regained consciousness, he realized what had happened and went home greatly saddened.

Sri Chaitanya Deva, the Supreme Lord residing in everyone's heart, was fully aware of all these events, but was reminded of them again another day when he saw Devananda in the street. He thought, "The disciples of such a guru will eventually become void of devotion, just like him." So he called out to him angrily:

"You there, Devananda Pandit! Listen, I have something to say to you. You lecture on the *Bhāgavatam*, don't you? Srivasa Thakur once came to hear your lecture. Your students dragged him out of your house while he was deeply absorbed in Krishna's pastimes. What was his offense? Was such manhandling a proper response to someone whose heart is saturated with bhakti rasa? Someone whose audience Ganga Devi herself craves? You may lecture on the *Bhāgavatam*, but you will never fathom its true import, not even after many lifetimes of trying. A person gets a certain amount of relief by going to the toilet after filling his belly. But I don't even get that kind of satisfaction when I hear the way you teach the *Bhāgavatam*, what to speak of the ecstasies of prema that are the real fruit of hearing it."

Devananda silently listened to the Lord's chastisement, which made him feel ashamed and dejected. Although Devananda was criticized in this way, he was truly a very fortunate soul because the Lord's chastisement is a rare blessing. Even demons who are slain by the Lord attain the spiritual realm of Vaikuntha. Anyone who faithfully and sincerely accepts the Supreme Lord's warnings or chastisements will soon be blessed with pure devotion to his lotus feet. Others who disregard the Lord's punishment revolve eternally in the material cosmos.

By chastising Devananda Pandit, Chaitanya Mahaprabhu teaches us a very important lesson: If one commits Vaishnava aparadh, then even if he endeavors to serve and surrender to Krishna, he will never attain prema because he is deprived of the blessings of the Vaishnavas.

After taking sannyasa, Mahaprabhu went to live in Jagannath Puri and only returned to Bengal one time thereafter. On that occasion, he visited the home of Sarvabhauma Bhattacharya's brother, Vidya Vachaspati, in Vidyanagar. From there he went to Chakuri Chattopadhyaya's house in Kuliya Gram, which also lies on the western bank of the Ganges. While there, a Brahmin came to meet the Lord. He held the Lord's lotus feet against his breast and pleaded:

"My Lord, kindly hear my plea. I am a notorious sinner. I have criticized Vaishnavas and the chanting of the Holy Name, thinking that there are no real Vaishnavas in Kali Yuga and doubting the power of Krishna's name. Now, my soul is burning from the memory of my misdeeds. You are the most powerful of personalities and have appeared just to save fallen persons like myself. Please, tell me what to do."

The Lord was pleased with the Brahmin's confession. Smiling, he said:

Mahaprabhu and the Maha Sankirtan Party

"O Brahmin, when nectar, the drink of immortality, is given to one who has been poisoned, the toxicity in his system gradually dissipates and his body becomes immortal. You have unwittingly drunk poison by criticizing Vaishnavas. The Holy Name of Krishna and his transcendental attributes are the highest nectar of immortality. You will only be forgiven if you constantly relish this nectar and glorify the Vaishnavas with the very tongue you used to criticize them. So glorify the wonderful qualities of Vaishnavas with song, poetry, or any other means and I will personally absolve you of your offenses and neutralize all of their poisonous effects.

"For one who unknowingly commits Vaishnava aparadh, the only recourse is to incessantly glorify the Vaishnavas and the Supreme Lord and simultaneously stop making further offenses. This is the only way to counteract the effects of aparadh. Penances and other practices are useless. So return to your home and delight in glorifying the Lord's devotees."

The assembled Vaishnavas were overjoyed to hear the Lord's merciful words, and they responded with resounding cries of "Hari! Hari!" Sri Gauranga instructs all unwitting Vaishnava aparadhis in the same way, and anyone who disregards these instructions and continues to offend and criticize sadhus is drowned in an ocean of sorrows. Those who take his advice, understanding that it is the cream of the Vedas, will easily cross over the vast sea of nescience and enter the eternal spiritual domain.

Srila Saraswati Thakur explains: "When the offender uses the same tongue that blasphemed the Vaishnava to express remorse and glorify the Vaishnava, it becomes auspicious. Poison gradually debilitates one's body functions, but the antidote brings the body back to its natural healthy condition. In the same way, to correct Vaishnava aparadh, neither avoiding further offenses nor millions of penances will be truly effective. Only honest and humble glorification of Vaishnavas can bring redemption.

"Those sinners who follow Mahaprabhu's instruction, believing it to be the infallible truth, who throw themselves at the Vaishnava's feet to beg forgiveness, reap enormous benefit. They develop unflinching

faith in Mahaprabhu and easily cross over the vast ocean of nescience."

Just as Mahaprabhu finished instructing the Brahmin, Devananda Pandit entered. Up to that moment, Devananda, despite his noble characteristics, had not been able to develop faith in the Lord or his teachings. In spite of extensive study and teaching of the *Śrīmad Bhāgavatam*, he had been unable to perceive its transcendental message of surrender to the Supreme Godhead. His heart was impaled by the desire for liberation, so he could not taste the sweetness of bhakti, nor could he teach bhakti to others.

After Mahaprabhu accepted sannyasa and left for Jagannath Puri, however, fate arranged for Devananda to meet Srila Vakresvara Pandit, a great devotee and an eternal associate of Chaitanya Mahaprabhu. This was a windfall of good fortune for Devananda. A pure devotee's association is like touchstone, so Devananda quickly developed *ruci* (spiritual taste) and an unassailable faith in Mahaprabhu.

Srila Vrindavan Das Thakur describes how the highly elevated Vaishnava Vakresvara Pandit came to Devananda's hermitage. Devananda was struck with wonder seeing his wonderful appearance and his ecstatic singing and dancing with deep emotion. The desire for liberation disappeared from his heart and he fell at Vakresvara's feet, smearing the dust all over his body. Reverence for Mahaprabhu blossomed within him, showing the wonderful result of serving a *mahā-bhāgavata* pure devotee.

Srila Saraswati Thakur writes: "As a direct result of service to a pure Vaishnava, unflinching faith in Mahaprabhu was aroused in the heart of Devananda Pandit. Vakresvara's taking up residence in Devananda's ashram brought immense good fortune to Devananda. Although Devananda was a ritualist, he was very learned and self-controlled. His studies of scripture were solely dedicated to *Śrīmad Bhāgavatam*. He was aloof from the dictates of his senses, but he lacked faith in Chaitanya Mahaprabhu. However, by Srila Vakresvara Pandit's grace, his misconceptions were eradicated and he developed regard for Mahaprabhu."

Srila Vrindavan Das Thakur writes: "Service to Vaishnavas is higher than service to the Lord. This is the verdict of the *Bhāgavatam* and all other revealed scriptures. The *Bhāgavatam* states: 'There may be doubts as to whether service to the Supreme Lord will give perfection or not, but there is absolutely no doubt about obtaining perfection by serving his devotees.' Thus, service to Vaishnavas is the most effective and sure method for everyone to reach Krishna."

(*Chaitanya Bhāgavata, Antya* 3.485-487)

Devananda Pandit's darshan of Mahaprabhu had a direct correlation to the purifying association of Vakresvara Pandit. Humility and all other Vaishnava attributes were manifest in Devananda as he prostrated himself at the Lord's lotus feet. He got up and meekly remained standing in a corner. The Lord was satisfied to see Devananda, and asked him to come and sit near him. The Lord had forgiven all his previous offenses and spoke to him intimately.

"You have had the great fortune of serving my beloved devotee. Vakresvara is a full-blown expansion of Krishna's shakti, or divine potency. Whoever serves him attains Krishna. His heart is Krishna's favorite resting place. Wherever he is becomes holy, and that place becomes my abode."

Devananda folded his palms and began to glorify the Lord: "O merciful Lord! You have appeared in Nabadwip to liberate everyone. I am miserable and fallen. Unfortunately I could not recognize you, and so I was deprived of the supreme bliss of your association and mercy. But it is your nature to be compassionate to all. I only pray that I may love you.

"But Lord, I have one request. Please tell me what to do. I am not omniscient, but the *Bhāgavatam* is meant for the all-knowing. How can an ignorant fool like me understand a book meant for the omniscient? And if I cannot understand it myself, how can I explain or teach it to others?"

Being pleased with Devananda, the Lord said: "Do not try to explain the *Bhāgavatam* in any way other than in the light of Krishna bhakti. From beginning to end the message of the *Bhāgavatam* is: love Krishna. In the entire material creation Krishna bhakti is the only absolute truth, and at the end of the world only this truth remains in all its potency. Narayan deceives the jivas by giving liberation and keeping bhakti hidden from them."

This is also stated in the *Chaitanya Charitāmṛta* (*Ādi* 8.18):

kṛṣṇa jadi chuṭe bhakte bhukti mukti diyā
tabu bhakti nā deya rākhen lukāiyā

"Krishna might eagerly give his devotee worldly pleasures or liberation, but he does not easily give devotion, preferring to keep it a secret."

This most rare jewel of devotion is a prize that can be had only through the mercy of Lord Krishna himself. The *Śrīmad Bhāgavatam* is the only scripture in which devotion to Krishna is established as the ultimate goal of existence. It is thus unlike any other. The *Bhāgavatam* is not a mundane composition; it is a transcendental literature that appears and disappears like the incarnations of God. It became manifest in this world on the tongue of Srila Vyasa Deva by Sri Krishna's mercy and by the transcendental potency of bhakti. Vrindavan Das Thakur warns that, since the *Bhāgavatam* is Krishna himself, one must not foolishly think that he knows and fully understands it.

The Lord continued: "Even if an ignorant person submissively approaches the *Bhāgavatam*, its purport is automatically revealed in his heart. Embodying pure spiritual love, the *Bhāgavatam* is one of Krishna's forms. All the sublime pastimes of Krishna are revealed within it. Although Veda Vyasa compiled the four Vedas, the Mahabharata, the Puranas and other literature, he felt empty and incomplete. But after compiling the *Bhāgavatam*, he felt completely satisfied. Yet there are those unfortunate souls who, even after reading this crest-jewel among the scriptures, are unable to taste the rich flavor of Krishna bhakti and remain under the thrall of ignorance.

"My dear Brahmin, simply emphasize bhakti when teaching the *Śrīmad Bhāgavatam*, whether at its beginning, middle or end. Then you will remain free from aparadh and your heart will fill with bliss. The essence of all scriptures is devotion to Krishna, but the *Bhāgavatam* is unique in that it is saturated with Krishna bhakti rasa. Splash the water from this ocean of nectar upon everyone."

Devananda Pandit was overwhelmed by Mahaprabhu's wonderful instructions. After offering obeisances at Mahaprabhu's lotus feet he left for his hermitage, filled with wonder at his good fortune.

Through his instructions to Devananda Pandit, Mahaprabhu broadcast the glories of *Śrīmad Bhāgavatam* to the world. The ultimate conclusion of the 18,000 verses of the *Bhāgavatam* is devotion to Krishna. That home which is graced by this auspicious literature is free from misfortune. Worship of *Śrīmad Bhāgavatam* is equal to worship of Krishna. Pure devotion to Krishna is obtained through regular hearing and recitation of this extraordinary book. Teaching any meaning other than bhakti is a waste of time and leads to aparadh.

There are two *Bhāgavatas*: *grantha-bhāgavata* — the book form of Divinity, and *bhakta-bhāgavata* — the devotee form of Divinity. Daily hearing, reciting, and worshipping of the *Bhāgavatam* results in realizing the truth about the Lord and his devotees. Srila Krishna Das Kaviraj writes:

eka bhāgavata baṛa bhāgavata śāstra
āra bhāgavata bhakta bhakti-rasa pātra

"One of the *Bhāgavatas* is the great scripture *Śrīmad Bhāgavatam*, and the other is the pure devotee who is absorbed in the mellows of loving devotion, rasa."
(*Chaitanya-caritāmṛta*, *Ādi* 1.99)

By constantly hearing, studying and worshiping the book *Bhāgavatam*, we will soon become devotee *bhāgavatas*; of this there can be no doubt.

Devananda Pandit became enlightened about the exalted position of Srivasa Thakur by receiving the mercy of Mahaprabhu and his eternal associate, Vakresvara Pandit. With heartfelt remorse and utmost humility he repeatedly begged forgiveness at Srivasa Thakur's lotus feet. Thus he received the blessings of Srivasa Thakur as well as all of Mahaprabhu's devotees.

The Lord says:

śabda-brahma paraṁ-brahma
mamobhe śāśvatī tanū

"The Supreme sound vibration and the Supreme Being are one and the same."

(*Śrīmad Bhāgavatam* 6.16.51)

No one is able to attract the mercy of the book *Bhāgavata* without first being blessed by the grace of the devotee *Bhāgavata*. Without this we remain forever incapable of relishing the nectar of Krishna bhakti. The slightest aparadh against the *bhakta-bhāgavata* will prevent anyone from achieving the mercy of the *Bhāgavatam*, the literary incarnation of God.

Sri Ganga Devi–Mother Ganges

Advaita Avatar

Sachi Ma & Her Nimai

Mahaprabhu will not tolerate any offense to his devotees regardless of who the offender is. In fact, once he was even displeased with his own mother, Sachi Devi, because she offended Advaita Acharya. Mahaprabhu said that until she begged the Acharya's forgiveness, she would never attain Krishna prema. Mahaprabhu used this incident to illustrate the dangers of committing offenses to the Holy Name, especially Vaishnava aparadh. This is truly an important and unique pastime, for how can the mother of God be denied Krishna prema? The special mercy of this pastime is that by hearing it faithfully, one develops the understanding to avoid Vaishnava aparadh. The details of this pastime are recorded in the *Madhya-khaṇḍa* of *Chaitanya Bhāgavata* as part of the *Mahāprakāśa-līlā* ("The Great Revelation").

One day Mahaprabhu sat on the deity throne, and gathered his expansions around him and said, "In the Kali Yuga, I am Krishna, I am Narayan, and I am Rama. One day I was floating on the milk ocean when Advaita Acharya's thunderous calls awakened me. I then descended at his request to inundate the world in a flood of Krishna prema."

Nityananda, the direct incarnation of Balaram, was in awe of Mahaprabhu's opulence and his magnanimous mood. He ran to his throne and held an umbrella above him. Gadadhara Pandit stood to Mahaprabhu's left and began to prepare tambul for the Lord. The other devotees surrounded him. Some began to fan him with chamaras. Like a desire tree, Mahaprabhu began to give devotion to everyone. They begged the Lord for devotion for themselves, for their mothers, their fathers, some for their gurus, for their disciples, and so on. Always ready to fulfill the wishes of his devotees, the Lord smiled and dispensed boons for attaining pure devotion.

Seeing that the Lord was inundating everyone with a flood of Krishna prema, Srivasa Pandit requested that Mahaprabhu shower prema bhakti on his mother, Sachi Devi. Mahaprabhu replied, "O Srivasa, do not make such a request. I will not offer her the ecstasy of divine love. She has committed Vaishnava aparadh and is being denied entry into the realm of divine love."

Srivasa Pandit was shocked and said, "Your words are like knives stabbing our hearts and killing us! Mother Sachi is the divine personality who has given birth to you. She is the devotees' sustaining life-force, the Universal Mother, and yet you refuse to give her prema? If this is one of your jokes, I think it has gone far enough. Now shower Mother Sachi with prema, my Lord. How can she possibly be guilty of Vaishnava aparadh? Even if you think that she is guilty, then kindly absolve her from it and give her your mercy."

The Lord replied: "I can advise on how to be forgiven for Vaishnava aparadh, but I cannot excuse an aparadh personally. The only way to be absolved of Vaishnava aparadh is to approach the offended Vaishnava and beg forgiveness, as in the case of the powerful sage Durvasa Muni, who committed offenses at the feet of the saintly King Ambarish. He was finally exonerated from his offense only when he approached that Vaishnava whom he had offended. Sachi Mata has committed an offense at the lotus feet of Advaita Acharya Prabhu and so she has to sprinkle the dust from his feet on her head and beg forgiveness. By his grace she will then receive my blessings in the form of prema, otherwise not."

> *"Mother Sachi is the Universal Mother, the embodiment of Vishnu bhakti. Her name is so potent that anyone uttering it will become free from all fears. The holy Ganges and Mother Sachi are nondifferent. Mother Sachi is the equal of Yashoda and Devaki."*

The point is that even the Supreme Lord himself cannot waive Vaishnava aparadh. The Lord's position is clear: "Although I am absolutely independent, I am dependent on my devotees. I am their captive. They are my heart and soul, and I am their heart and soul. I always protect them, and they are willing to die for me."

Therefore, how can the Lord forgive an offender of his beloved devotees? The only recourse for the offender is to throw himself at the feet of the Vaishnava he has offended and beg forgiveness. When the compassionate Vaishnava forgives the offender, then the Lord, who relishes the magnanimity of his devotees, becomes pleased with the offender and blesses him.

As soon as the devotees heard the Lord's instructions, they ran to Advaita Acharya Prabhu and narrated everything to him. Hearing the Lord's instructions, Advaita Acharya was astounded. He said to the devotees: "I'm ruined. Are you trying to kill me? Don't you realize Mother Sachi's supramundane position? My beloved Lord has appeared from her womb; she is my mother too. I consider it my great fortune to humbly receive the dust of her feet. She is the Universal Mother, the embodiment of Vishnu bhakti. I am surprised that all of you are unaware of her spiritual potency and talk like this. Her name is so potent that anyone uttering it, even if under the illusion that it is a mundane sound, will become free from all fears. The holy Ganges and Mother Sachi are nondifferent. Mother Sachi is the equal of Yashoda and Devaki."

While glorifying the divine attributes of Mother Sachi Devi, Sri Advaita Acharya became ecstatic and fainted. Mother Sachi came out of hiding and quickly smeared Advaita's foot-dust on her head. Unable to contain her intense rapture, she lost consciousness and fell to the ground. Thus an amazing situation arose in which Advaita was in a state of trance, meditating on Sachi's glories, while Sachi was similarly in a trance of concentration on Advaita Prabhu.

At that moment Mahaprabhu began to laugh very loudly, extremely satisfied with his mother. He said: "Now I will bless you with devotion to Vishnu. All your offenses to Advaita Prabhu have been absolved." Hearing these words, the devotees began cheering and rejoicing.

In this way, Lord Gaurasundara used his own mother as an example to instruct everyone on the immense gravity and danger of committing Vaishnava aparadh. Vrindavan Das focuses our attention on this crucial point: "If someone even as powerful as Lord Shiva offends a Vaishnava, then according to the scriptures he is destroyed. As for those foolish persons who are ignorant of this fact and commit Vaishnava aparadh, they must suffer untold pains, birth after birth. Even the Supreme Lord Gaurasundara's mother was not spared the reaction for committing Vaishnava aparadh."

Srila Saraswati Thakur writes in his purport: "If even the Supreme Lord's mother —most blessed among

Sachi fears Vishvambhar will leave home

women — had to face the consequences of Vaishnava aparadh, one can only imagine the outcome for an ordinary soul."

In analyzing Mother Sachi's alleged offense, her deep sorrow caused by separation from her son must be taken into consideration. Obviously, she did not really commit an offense, yet Sri Mahaprabhu condemned her action as offensive and denied her prema bhakti.

Mother Sachi's apparent offense to Sri Advaita Prabhu must certainly be explained. Previously, her eldest son Visvarupa had become completely detached from material life and accepted sannyasa under the influence of Advaita Acharya. When she saw her younger son Visvambhara similarly becoming aloof from family affairs, Mother Sachi was worried and began to think that Advaita Acharya was encouraging him to leave home as well.

Visvarupa was Mahaprabhu's elder brother, the expansion of Balaram and Nityananda. He is also Lord Maha Sankarshan of Vaikuntha. He was extraordinarily beautiful and effulgent, the embodiment of all scriptural conclusions and extremely equipoised. Nabadwip, the seat of scholarship in India at the time, did not have a single scholar who could fathom the depth of Visvarupa's learning, yet he played like an ordinary boy with his friends.

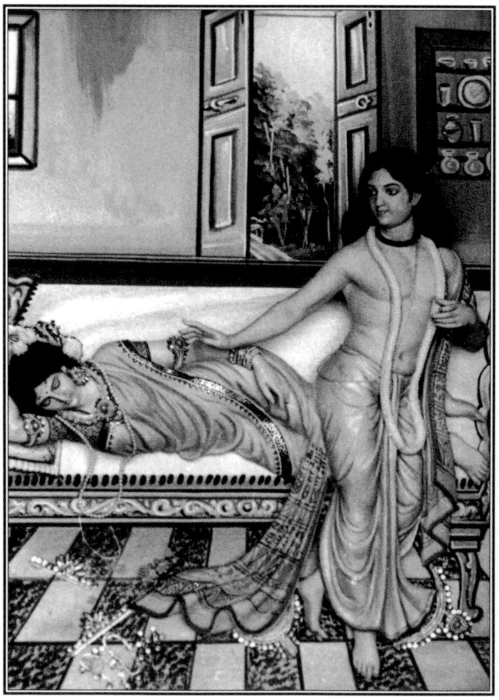
Nimai Pundit leaves home

One day Visvarupa's father, Sri Jagannath Mishra, took him to an assembly of pandits who were very pleased to see him. His exquisite beauty charmed and captivated everyone. One pandit asked Visvarupa, "My dear son, what are you studying?" Sri Visvarupa replied, "I have made a little progress in understanding all subjects." Considering him to be a mere boy, the pandit deferred from further questioning, but Jagannath Mishra felt ashamed that his son had not made a better showing.

When he had finished his business there, Jagannath took his son home. On the way he boxed Visvarupa's ears and reprimanded him. "Why didn't you name the books that you have studied? Everyone must have thought that you are stupid. You made me look like a fool." Jagannath continued to chastise Visvarupa all the way home.

Once there, however, Visvarupa slipped out of the house and returned to the assembly. He addressed the pandits and said, "When I was here earlier, you did not ask me any specific questions about my studies, so I gave you a general answer, but my father chastised me for appearing foolish. So now if anyone has any specific question, please ask it." One of the pandits inquired, "Please explain in detail what you learned today." Visvarupa began by presenting a thesis, then strongly refuted it with an antithesis, and then established another argument in favor of the first. The pandits were amazed and praised him profusely.

Though the teachers and pandits regularly studied and lectured on the *Bhagavad-gītā* and *Śrīmad Bhāgavatam*, their explanations were devoid of bhakti. A general lack of devotion among the residents of Nabadwip caused great distress to the young Visvarupa. The sole exception to this rule was the regular assemblies held in Advaita Acharya's house, where all scriptures were discussed in the light of Krishna bhakti. These assemblies gave immense pleasure to Visvarupa and so he spent long hours listening to the spiritual conclusions discussed

Brahma and all of the Gods pray for the Supreme Lord to descend

there. Often Mother Sachi would send Visvambhara to call Visvarupa home for prasad. Visvambhara's appearances in these assemblies brought joy to everyone.

Gradually Visvarupa lost interest in the world and family affairs. He left home and took sannyasa, after which he was known as Sripada Shankararanya. He traveled throughout India and eventually left the world in Pandharpur in Maharashtra. Visvarupa's departure was a source of constant pain in Sachi Mata's heart. The pain of separation and the thought that Advaita Acharya had been the cause of Visvarupa leaving home constantly troubled her mind, but she kept her feelings inside, fearing Vaishnava aparadh. Instead, she would embrace Nimai and silently bear the torment of Visvarupa's absence.

Then her darling Nimai also began to spend long hours at Advaita Acharya's house. He began to neglect his beautiful young wife Lakshmipriya. Seeing this, Mother Sachi became extremely apprehensive. He was her youngest son and the only one she had left. Now, he too had begun to withdraw from the family.

In her anguish Mother Sachi lamented: "Has Advaita Acharya stolen this son of mine as well? Who says he is Advaita? To me he is *dvaita*, a double-dealer. He has already driven away my first beautiful son with the moon-like face. Now he won't allow my only other boy to settle down at home. I feel so alone; no one has any sympathy for me. To the world he may be the famous Advaita, but for me he is *dvaita*, or the creator of separation."

This is all there was to Mother Sachi's offense and yet the Supreme Lord Gaurasundara refused to bless her with prema bhakti. The Supreme Lord's own mother merely thought offensive things and never even expressed them aloud, but she was denied bhakti by the Lord. Just imagine what happens to an ordinary person who openly offends the sadhu, guru, or Vaishnava. Simply thinking about it makes one shudder. Therefore devotees must be extremely cautious. By the Lord's will, this pastime was enacted to emphasize the severity of committing Vaishnava aparadh and the urgency of having it absolved.

Elsewhere, Vrindavan Das Thakur writes: "Lord Gaurachandra, the soul of the universe, delivered Jagai and Madhai, and the merciful Lord saved everyone except the Vaishnava-blasphemers, who are considered the worst. Blasphemy against the Lord's devotees is a horrendous offense. According to scripture, even if the offender is as powerful as Lord Shiva, the consequences are severe."

In the *Śrīmad Bhāgavatam*, King Rahugana says to Jada Bharata: "I have committed a grievous offense by insulting a great devotee like yourself. I, who am as powerful as Lord Shiva, shall be vanquished without delay for offending the lotus feet of a Vaishnava."

Even if the offender is extremely learned, he will be hurled down to the lowest hell. The holy name of Krishna is the most potent of purifying agents, but the Vaishnava-offender cannot be acquitted of his offense even by chanting the Holy Name. Blasphemy or criticism of saintly persons is the most damaging offense a person can commit against the Holy Name. The holy name of God *is* God, the Nāma Prabhu.

The *Padma-purāṇa* states that to be exonerated of one's sins, the purifying power of the Holy Name is far more potent than all the methods of penances recom-

Jagai and Madhai receive Mahaprabhu's mercy

mended in the scriptures. However, not even the Holy Name can protect one who offends or blasphemes a devotee of the Lord. When Vaishnava aparadh is committed, the offender cannot benefit from *nāmābhāsa* or from *śuddha-nāma* until he is absolved of his offenses.

At Yudhisthira Maharaja's *rājasūya-yajña* (royal sacrifice), a debate arose about who in the assembly should be the first to receive worship. The youngest of the Pandavas, Sahadeva, immediately pointed to Krishna, the Supreme Lord of lords. Krishna's avowed enemy, Sisupala, could not bear to have Krishna receive such glorification and began a tirade of abuses against him. The entire assembly was shocked. The *Śrīmad Bhāgavatam* describes how the members of the assembly covered their ears in disgust and marched angrily out of the hall. If upon hearing blasphemy one does not leave immediately, he becomes a party to it, loses all piety and goes to hell.

Sisupala, unfazed by the departure of the followers of Krishna, began insulting them and picked up his sword. Krishna tried to pacify and restrain his followers, but when he saw Sisupala rushing toward him with his sword drawn, he released his Sudarshan disc and cut off his head. Sisupala's supporters ran for their lives. As Sisupala breathed his last, a brilliant ray of light from Sisupala's body merged into Krishna's transcendental body, but not a drop of blood was shed, so the sacrifice continued, uncontaminated.

Shortly after this incident, another demon named Dantavakra was slain by Krishna and was liberated. Sisupala and Dantavakra were actually the third and final incarnations of the eternal associates of Narayan, Jaya and Vijaya. With their deaths they were eligible to return to Vaikuntha. Krishna, the Lord of yajnas (Yajnesvara), stayed and protected the sanctity of the sacrifice until its conclusion.

The *Chaitanya Bhāgavata* describes the famous incident of Jagai and Madhai offending Nityananda Prabhu and how they were subsequently saved. "Two notorious brothers, Jagai and Madhai, committed every conceivable immoral act, but they had never blasphemed a Vaishnava. Because they were always drunk, they never knew what they were doing and so somehow they avoided offending devotees. Even the most sacred assembly loses its sanctity with the slightest criticism of pure devotees. In fact, a party of rogues (dacoits) is far better than such an unholy assembly. At least a rogue still has a chance someday to be excused for his sinful behavior, but an offender is bound for hell."

Sri Bhaktisiddhanta Saraswati Prabhupada comments, "If we make the mistake of engaging in fault-finding and criticizing others, indulging our baser instincts, we drag our souls down. Without being free from envy, no one can climb out of this inauspicious abyss. Mahaprabhu liberated drunkards and debauchees, but rejected anyone who offended his devotees. Fault-finding can never enhance one's devotion or spiritual realization; it simply brings severe reactions. This is one of the reasons why great souls avoid criticizing anyone, especially devotees."

(*Chaitanya Bhāgavata Madhya* 13.311-312)

"An ignorant fool who first worships a Brahmin's feet and then kicks him on the head paves his way to hell. Similarly, one who worships the deity of Vishnu but does not revere the presence of Vishnu within every living being also goes to hell." (*Nārada-pañcarātra*)

"Setting aside Vaishnava aparadh, if anyone harasses even an ordinary living being, he must suffer severe consequences. If a person worships the deity of Vishnu but torments his creation, he does not benefit from his worship and experiences terrible agony. Such a person is ignorant of the truth that Lord Vishnu resides in all living beings. The horrible results of Vaishnava aparadh are a thousand times worse than offending a non-Vaishnava.

"A person who worships the deity but does not respect the Lord's devotees; or who is not compassionate to the fallen people; or who worships one aspect of divinity and not others, making mundane distinctions between Krishna and Ramachandra; or who does not revere Balaram or Shiva, is designated

Jagai & Madhai are delivered

in the scriptures as a third-class devotee."
(*Chaitanya Bhāgavata*, 2.5.140-149)

Śrīmad Bhāgavatam states: "One may give up bad association, take initiation, and worship the deity in the temple, but if he does not worship the devotees he is nothing more than a pseudo-Vaishnava."

"One who has taken initiation in the Vishnu-mantra and is worshipping Vishnu's deity with faith is a Vaishnava; others are non-Vaishnavas."
(*Padma-purāṇa* 1.55)

A devotee of Vishnu is a Vaishnava, and the Supreme Lord, who is the protector of his devotees, will not tolerate any blasphemy against such devotees. If we want to enter the Lord's heart the only passage is through the hearts of his devotees.

" Mahaprabhu liberated drunkards and debauchees, but rejected anyone who offended His devotees. Fault-finding can never enhance one's devotion or spiritual realization; it simply brings severe reactions. This is one of the reasons why great souls avoid criticizing anyone, especially devotees. "

VAISHNAVA APARADH

The Path of Spiritual Caution

ONCE, A BRAHMIN POET WROTE A PLAY about Sri Chaitanya Mahaprabhu. He went to the holy city of Jagannath Puri to see an old friend and associate of Mahaprabhu, Sri Bhagavan Acharya. The poet wanted him to hear the play and so he read it aloud to the acharya and a gathering of Vaishnavas. They praised the composition and thought that Mahaprabhu himself would be pleased to hear it.

But before anything was read to Mahaprabhu it was first presented to his secretary and confidante Svarupa Damodar. This was to ensure that the spiritual exchanges of rasa presented in the composition were not distasteful, or that the esoteric principles of devotion were not misinterpreted. If such faulty writing were presented to the Lord, he would become deeply disturbed.

Bhagavan Acharya approached Svarupa Damodar and requested that he read the composition first and then present it to Mahaprabhu. In Krishna lila, Svarupa Damodar is Lalita Sakhi, the principal confidante of Srimati Radharani and therefore most expert in the science of rasa. Knowing that the poet was a pure and simple Vaishnava, Svarupa Damodar gently chastised him:

"My dear Bhagavan Acharya, you are a very generous Vrindavan cowherd boy and the desire to read any literature presented as scripture sometimes overpowers you. When unqualified poets write about rasa, their poetry does not arouse the desired emotion when heard; it is *rasābhāsa*, a mere semblance of rasa. Such writing is contrary to spiritual reality. Anyone who cannot properly identify and mix *rasika* mellows will forever be on the shore of the *bhakti-siddhānta-sindhu*. He is fooling himself and others. Mahaprabhu's pastimes are particularly difficult to grasp, so only persons who have enshrined Mahaprabhu's lotus feet within their hearts as their life and soul are qualified to narrate Krishna lila and Gaura lila.

"Mundane love stories sadden me, but the writings of an expert devotee steeped in ecstatic love bring great joy. Srila Rupa Goswami has set the standard for writing drama. Simply hearing the introductory passages to his two plays, *Vidagdha-mādhava* and *Lalita-mādhava*, gives one great spiritual pleasure."

Despite Svarupa Damodar's caution, Bhagavan Acharya repeatedly requested that he read the poem at least once before making a judgment. After repeated entreaties, Svarupa Damodar reluctantly agreed. He assembled all the Vaishnavas and sat down to listen to the drama about Mahaprabhu. The poet read the *nāndī-śloka* (benedictory prologue) to his play:

vikaca-kamala-netre śrī-jagannātha-saṁjñe
kanaka-rucir ihātmany ātmatāṁ yaḥ prapannaḥ
prakṛti-jaḍam aśeṣaṁ cetayann āvirāsīt
sa diśatu tava bhavyaṁ kṛṣṇa-caitanya-devaḥ

"The Supreme Personality of Godhead who radiates a golden complexion has become the soul of the body named Jagannath. His lotus eyes are in full bloom. He has appeared in Jagannath Puri and brought dull matter to life. May that Lord, Sri Krishna Chaitanya Deva, bestow all good fortune upon you."
(*Chaitanya Charitāmṛta Antya* 5.116)

After he had finished reading this verse, everyone praised the composition. Svarupa Damodar, however, asked the poet to explain its meaning. The Brahmin said, "Lord Jagannath's body is exquisite and beautiful and Mahaprabhu is the soul of that body. Mahaprabhu has appeared in Nilachala, Jagannath Puri, to awaken the spiritual consciousness of the 'soulless' material world."

In spite of the approval of the group, Svarupa Damodar was outraged and said: "You fool! Are you trying to destroy yourself? Have you no faith in either of these forms of the Lord? Jagannath is the embodiment of transcendence and absolute spiritual bliss, yet you have described his body as material, dull and inert. And you have described Mahaprabhu, the Supreme Reality, as though he were an ordinary mortal. He is the 'Supreme Fire' from whom everything emanates; yet you have portrayed him as a mere spark. So you have offended both Jagannath and Mahaprabhu and are doomed. Even hell isn't good enough for you. Those who are ignorant of the principles of divine love yet dare to comment on them are fools!

"You are in total illusion. You have discriminated between the body and soul of the Supreme Personality of Godhead. This is a great offense. There is absolutely no distinction between the body and soul of the Supreme Lord. The Lord's personal identity and his body are one and the same."

Svarupa Damodar then quoted a sloka from the *Kūrma-purāṇa* also found in the *Laghu-bhāgavatāmṛta* of Rupa Goswami: "There is never any difference between the body and soul of the Supreme Godhead."

He continued, "Krishna is the Lord of the deluding energy Maya. He is the absolute embodiment of spiritual opulence and infinite bliss, whereas the living entity is infinitesimal and is always suffering as the slave of Maya. Like Vishnu Swami says, 'The Supreme Lord has a transcendental body full of ecstasy, embraced by his pleasure-giving and spiritual potencies. The jiva, by contrast, is immersed in ignorance of himself and therefore submerged in misery and suffering.'"

When the Vaishnavas heard Svarupa Damodar, the master of subtle philosophical analysis, admonish the poet from Bengal, they were stunned. The poet him-

Krishna instruct His friend and devotee, Arjuna, on the battlefield

self was extremely ashamed and apprehensive and, feeling like a buzzard among swans, he hung his head. Svarupa Damodar was moved by the poet's dejection and said sweetly:

"Go and study *Śrīmad Bhāgavatam* from a Vaishnava and take complete shelter of Mahaprabhu's lotus feet. Always seek the association of Mahaprabhu's devotees; only then will you be able to navigate the waves of the ocean of devotion. Everything will be revealed to you. Then you can be a real pandit and describe Krishna lila without fault."

We should note that Mother Saraswati, the goddess of learning, transforms the deluded ravings of those who are devoid of proper spiritual understanding into eulogies of her Lord, Sri Krishna. Thus Svarupa Damodar was able to interpret the poet's verse in a way that conformed to the *siddhānta* accepted by Mahaprabhu:

"There is no difference between Jagannath and Krishna, but in Puri, Jagannath is unmoving, fixed in one place as the infinite appearing in wood. Jagannath and Mahaprabhu, although appearing separately, are one because they are the same Krishna in two forms. The desire to deliver the world burns inside their hearts. To save everyone, Krishna descended as Sri Chaitanya Mahaprabhu. By seeing Jagannath, one is freed from material existence; but not everyone can be admitted into his temple in Jagannath Puri to see him. Chaitanya Mahaprabhu, however, moves from one country to another, personally or through his representatives. In this way he delivers all the people of the world."

The Brahmin understood his mistakes and with great humility begged for shelter at the feet of all the

Vaishnavas. The Vaishnavas were moved and arranged for him to meet Mahaprabhu personally. The poet later took sannyasa and continued to live in Puri. So we see that in order to receive the Lord's mercy, we must first obtain the mercy of his devotees.

Vishnu and Vaishnavas, or Krishna and the *Kārṣṇas* are beyond mundane scrutiny. Krishna says in the *Bhagavad-gītā*:

avajānanti māṁ mūḍhā
mānuṣīṁ tanum āśritam
paraṁ bhāvam ajānanto
mama bhūta-maheśvaram

"Fools think that I am an ordinary human being, or at most that God may have descended in a bag of flesh; but I am transcendental — body and soul — the Supreme Controller of everything."

(*Bhagavad-gītā* 9.11)

It is stated in the *Śrī Chaitanya Charitāmṛta*: "Although God has innumerable forms and pastimes, his highest pastimes are performed as Krishna, appearing in human form, dressed as an ever-youthful cowherd boy, dancing brilliantly and playing on his flute."

(*Chaitanya Charitāmṛta, Madhya* 21.101)

The Supreme Personality of Godhead is the fully independent Lord and the master of unlimited potencies. As the controller of Maya he uses his spiritual illusion (*yogamāyā-śakti*) to assist him in manifesting his pastimes in the world. Although these pastimes appear to be mundane, they are supramundane:

"The transcendental form of Krishna, as revealed by

Krishna's internal spiritual energy, is the secret treasure of the devotees. This form is manifest from Krishna's eternal pastimes in the spiritual domain."
(*Chaitanya Charitāmṛta, Madhya* 21.103)

The Goddess Saraswati

To consider the infinite Supreme Lord on the same level with the finite jiva soul, or to distinguish between the Supreme Lord's body and soul as if he were an ordinary person, is to come under the influence of the warped Mayavada philosophy. Krishna condemns the Mayavadi's failure to accept his eternal, infinite, blissful body.

Srila Visvanath Chakravarti Thakur introduces the next *Gītā* verse by asking, "What becomes of those who think that the Lord's body is matter?" It is in expectation of such a question that Krishna says,

moghāśā mogha-karmāṇo
mogha-jñāna vicetasaḥ
rākṣāsīṁ āsuriṁ caiva
prakṛtiṁ mohinīṁ śritāḥ

"Those who deny the existence of God seek shelter in the world. But ultimately their hopes and aspirations, their advancement of science and technology, leave them empty, confused and lost." (*Bhagavad-gītā* 9.12)

"If these offenders are devotees there is a different meaning. That their hopes and aspirations are crushed means, their thirst for liberation (*sālokya*) is unattainable. If they are karmis (fruitive workers), they are deprived of being elevated to the heavenly planets (Svarga-loka). As for jnanis (philosophers), they cannot obtain moksha or *sāyujya* (liberation of merging with Brahman). Then what do they actually gain? They acquire a demonic mentality and nature and end up hating the Lord and his devotees."

The *Bhagavad-gītā* states:

mahātmānas tu māṁ pārtha
daiviṁ prakṛtim āśritāḥ
bhajanty ananya-manaso
jñātvā bhūtādim avyayam

"On the other hand, the really great souls of this world are those who have completely taken shelter in me. Under the direction of my superior energy they are constantly absorbed in loving me, knowing that I am the inexhaustible source of everything."
(*Bhagavad-gītā* 9.13)

These great souls realize that although the Supreme Lord appears in human-like form, he is the embodiment of *sat, cit* and *ānanda* and is indestructible and infinite. This *ananya-manaḥ*, or constant absorption in bhajan, is the *rāja-guhyaṁ* — the king of all secrets. The following sloka from the *Gītā* elaborates on the nature of bhajan:

satataṁ kīrtayanto māṁ
yatantaś ca dṛḍha-vratāḥ
namasyantaś ca māṁ bhaktyā
nitya-yuktā upāsate

"Always absorbed in kirtan, with the greatest sense of purpose, my devotees are bowed before me perpetually worshipping me." (*Bhagavad-gītā* 9.14)

Generally speaking, the devotees must observe the rules and regulations of devotion. However, the *Viṣṇu-dharma* states that: "In chanting the Lord's name there is no consideration of time and place."

In the aforementioned *Bhagavad-gītā* sloka, the Lord deliberately hints at *rāgānugā bhakti*. The behavior of a *rāga-bhakta* may bewilder those in the lower stages of devotion, so the scriptures warn that such mahatmas, or great souls, must never be judged according to mundane considerations:

"A person who considers the deity of the Lord to be a statue, or the guru and Vaishnavas as ordinary people belonging to a particular social class or caste; the foot-bath water of Vishnu or the Vaishnavas as dirty water; the all-purifying holy name of Vishnu or Krishna as mundane sound; or the Supreme Lord of lords, Hari, as being on the same level as the gods, is a resident of hell."
(*Padma-purāṇa*)

Mahaprabhu has confirmed that eternal service to Krishna is our real occupation:

jīvera svarūpa hay kṛṣṇera nitya-dāsa

"The jiva's inherent identity is that he is the eternal servant of Krishna."
(*Chaitanya Charitāmṛta, Madhya* 20.108)

The deluded jiva is in forgetfulness of his real identity. Thus he becomes completely absorbed in family, making money, pursuing mundane education and physical beauty (*janma, aiśvarya, śruta, śrī*). These four feed his pride and often precede offensive actions against Vishnu and the Vaishnavas.

Sri Parankush Muni[1] says that indifference to four particular qualities of the Lord's incarnation in the Deity form propels the jiva towards committing the aparadh of *arcye viṣṇau śilā-dhīr*, or seeing the deity of the Lord as an ordinary sculpture. These four qualities are explained as follows:

(1) *Saulabhya* ("accessibility") means the Lord's facility of obtention. In other words, the Lord appears on Earth in his deity form for all of us to see, so that we may easily take shelter of him.

(2) *Sauśīlya* ("excellence of disposition"), by which the Lord erases the devotee's fear of approaching him on account of the vast difference between them;

(3) *Svāmitva* ("mastership") is that quality of the Lord that gives the jiva confidence that the Lord will fulfill all of his desires.

(4) *Vātsalya* ("tenderness") is that quality of the Lord by which he puts an end to the devotee's trembling when he thinks of his shortcomings.[2]

If a disciple does not hear attentively from the spiritual master about the five forms in which the Lord appears to the jiva, his faith will slowly lose strength. These five forms are:

(1) *Para* ("supreme"), i.e. the Lord's original form in his eternal abode;

(2) *Vyūha* ("emanation"), i.e., the Lord's primary expansions, Vasudeva, Sankarshan, Pradyumna and Aniruddha, who are engaged in the work of creation;

(3) *Vaibhava* ("manifestation"), i.e., the Lord's incarnations in this world;

(4) *Antaryāmī* ("inner controller"), the form of the Lord that dwells in the heart of every creature; and

(5) *Arcā* ("image"), i.e., the form of the Lord as the deity in the temple.[3]

The jiva must cultivate a positive outlook and give up bad association while seeking the company of pure devotees. Desire leads to bad association, which influences the jiva to develop an atheistic mentality. The scriptures implore us to keep good association:

"Deceiving oneself and others is called *kaitava*.

Associating with people who are lying to themselves is called *duḥsaṅga* (bad association). Those who think that things other than service to Krishna will satisfy them are also called *duḥsaṅga*."

"A person must reject bad association and keep the company of genuine devotees. They tell us how to cut the knots of attachment to things bad for devotion."

It is stated in the *Bhakti-sandarbha* that even one's guru is unworthy of association if he shows enmity towards Vaishnavas. The scriptures instruct that such mundane gurus, whether instructors in a worldly sense, or spiritual guides by virtue of family custom or some other contingency, must be abandoned in favor of a bone fide guru.

Bad association of any kind must be avoided like disease:

"The proper conduct for a Vaishnava is to avoid materialistic company. Generally speaking, there are two types of *duḥsaṅga* or *asat-saṅga*: persons who are slaves to their senses and those who are not devotees or do not accept Krishna."

According to this statement a sincere soul must avoid *asat-saṅga* and always seek the association of pure devotees; otherwise devotional endeavors bear no fruit. Bad association results in aparadh. Vaishnava aparadh and *guru-avajñā*, disobeying the guru, are the two most serious offenses. The devotee must strive to surround himself by the protective wall of sadhu sanga or saintly association.

A sincere devotee will carefully abstain from indulging in any disparaging thoughts about a Vaishnava's external qualifications. This is particularly important regarding exalted persons who are the real saviors of mankind, but even a neophyte who has recently taken shelter of a Vaishnava guru should be respected and must not be judged by mundane standards. Vrindavan Das Thakur writes that even a veteran Vaishnava has to suffer the consequences for disrespecting another Vaishnava.

Even a person born a Brahmin due to previous pious deeds does not have a right to act or speak arrogantly or to harbor disparaging thoughts about a Vaishnava. Such thoughts will cause chaos in his life. He becomes controlled by lust, greed and anger and madly chases after women, fame and fortune. He becomes totally absorbed in material life and his attachments so thickly cover his vision that even death cannot open his eyes to the truth of the hell that awaits him.

We have seen how a powerful yogi like Saubhari Rishi had to succumb to material allurements due to his aparadh against Garuda and Prajapati Daksha had to suffer untold misery because of his offenses to Shiva. Many incidents of such offenses and their dramatic consequences can be found in Mahaprabhu's pastimes also. Devananda Pandit and Gopal Chapal offended Srivasa Thakur, the purest of devotees, and Ramachandra Khan and the Brahmin Gopal Chakravarti offended the most exalted Vaishnava Hari Das Thakur; all these offenders experienced horrendous miseries.

Vaishnava aparadh can be absolved only when the

offended Vaishnava chooses to forgive the offender. Serving a different Vaishnava or begging the Supreme Lord for forgiveness will not excuse him. We also saw how the great mystic Durvasa Muni offended the magnanimous King Ambarish and was harassed by the avowed protector of Vaishnavas, Sudarshan Chakra. Even the Supreme Lord could not pardon his offenses; Durvasa Muni had to return to the Vaishnava he offended and only after surrendering at King Ambarish's feet were his offenses excused.

An offender may chant and perform acts of devotion, but they are merely play-acting: in a million lifetimes they will not bear the fruit of devotion. What is the use of such bhajan and sadhana if the only medium through which Krishna's mercy descends is denigrated? It is impossible to receive the Supreme Lord's grace if the blessings of the guru and the Vaishnava are ignored.

The Supreme Lord is *bhakta-vatsala*, the guardian of devotees. He does not pay the slightest heed to the prayers of such offenders. Deprived of the Lord's grace, they become subjected to demoniac and atheistic mentalities that gradually degrade their nature and they become a burden to the world.

During a discussion between Mahaprabhu and Ramananda Raya, Mahaprabhu inquired: "Of all that is good and beneficial to the jiva, what brings him the optimum benefit?" Ramananda Raya replied: "For the jiva, there is no greater benefit than *kṛṣṇa-bhakta-saṅga*, or association with Krishna's pure devotees."

(*Chaitanya Charitāmṛta, Madhya-līlā* 8.251)

Mahaprabhu also instructed everyone through Sanatan Goswami: "A person born outside of India is not unfit for devotion to Krishna, nor is one considered fit for devotion simply because he is born in a family of Brahmins. Anyone who takes to devotional service is exalted, whereas a sworn non-devotee is always condemned. Therefore, in devotional service to the Lord, there is no consideration of family status. Krishna is always extremely kind to the meek and humble, whereas aristocrats and learned scholars are too proud of their material qualifications."

"Among the various acts of devotion, nine-fold (*nava-vidhā*) bhakti is the best as it bestows ecstatic love for Krishna. Of those nine limbs of bhakti, chanting the Lord's holy name is foremost. If one chants without committing the ten offenses, he obtains the treasure of love of God."

(*Chaitanya Charitāmṛta, Antya-līlā* 4.66-71)

By birth, Brahmins possess sole rights to perform sacrifices, penance and austerities. But they also seek elevation to the heavenly planets, which are undesirable to a devotee of Krishna. Among the general population, however, the Brahmins are still considered to be the elite and so it behooves us to remember the dictum, *bhaktau nṛ-mātrasyādhikārita*: not only human beings, but every living entity has a God-given right to engage in bhakti. Therefore a Vaishnava devotee, even if born in the West, is accepted as the best of Brahmins in a spiritual society. However, if one is a Brahmin by birth and is a non-devotee, then he is considered very degraded:

"If a meat-eater becomes a devotee of the Supreme Lord Hari, he is far superior to a Brahmin, but if a Brahmin has no devotion, he is worse than a meat-eater."

Sri Chaitanya & his intimate associate Ramananda Raya

The most effective religious practice in the present age of Kali Yuga is the sankirtan yajna, or singing of the holy name of Krishna under the guidance of pure devotees. Hence, anyone who is initiated into this process of Nāma yajna is elevated among humankind.

The *Śrīmad Bhāgavatam*, the fully ripened fruit of the tree of Vedic knowledge, concludes that only one possessed of superior intellect can grasp that the sankirtan yajna is the sole means in Kali Yuga to worship the Supreme Lord. Instruction on the process of sankirtan yajna and *nava-vidhā bhakti* abound in the *Śrīmad Bhāgavatam*:

kṛṣṇa-varṇaṁ tviṣākṛṣṇaṁ
sāṅgopāṅgāstra-pārṣadam
yajñaiḥ saṅkirtan-prāyair,
yajanti hi su-medhasaḥ

"In the age of Kali, the most intelligent persons worship Sri Chaitanya Mahaprabhu and sing the holy name of Krishna. Although Mahaprabhu's complexion is not blackish like Krishna's, he is nonetheless Krishna himself. He is accompanied by his associates, servants, weapons and confidential companions. Real intelligence means to worship Krishna exclusively."

(*Śrīmad Bhāgavatam* 11.5.32)

Below are three slokas that clearly emphasize the efficacy of the three main devotional activities of hearing, chanting and remembrance:

tasmād ekena manasā
bhagavān sātvatāṁ patiḥ
śrotavyaḥ kīrtitavyaś ca
dhyeyaḥ pūjyaś ca nityadā

"Being completely focused, one should constantly hear about, glorify, remember and worship Bhagavan Sri Krishna, who is the guardian of his devotees."

(*Śrīmad Bhāgavatam* 1.2.14)

tasmāt sarvātmanā rājan
hariḥ sarvatra sarvadā
śrotavyaḥ kīrtitavyaś ca
smartavyo bhagavān nṛṇām

"It is essential that every human being hear about, glorify and remember Krishna always and everywhere."

(*Śrīmad Bhāgavatam* 2.2.36)

tasmād bhārata sarvātmā
bhagavān īśvaro hariḥ
śrotavyaḥ kīrtitavyaś ca
smartavyaś cecchatābhayam

"One who wants to be free from this miserable existence must hear about, glorify and remember Krishna, who is the Supersoul, the Supeme Controller and our savior from all miseries." (*Śrīmad Bhāgavatam* 2.1.5)

The next sloka establishes that Nāma sankirtan is the best means for success whether one is a karmi, jnani, or yogi:

etan nirvidyamānānām
icchatām akuto-bhayam
yogīnāṁ nṛpa nirṇītaṁ
harer nāmānukīrtanam

"O King Pariksit, the only process for the yogis who are free from material desire and wish to become completely fearless is to take shelter of the holy name of Krishna under the guidance of a pure devotee." This verse indicates that karmis, jnanis or yogis should all take up the chanting of the Holy Name to achieve their own goals." (*Śrīmad Bhāgavatam* 2.1.11)

Srila Jiva Goswami points out in the *Bhakti-sandarbha* that of the various kinds of kirtan — chanting the Supreme Lord's name, qualities, beauty and pastimes — the chanting of the Holy Name is the greatest. The *Bhāgavatam* explains that the highest religious principle for humanity is to be completely and irresistibly devoted to Krishna, for this alone will completely satisfy the soul (*ātmā suprasīdati*). Elsewhere in the *Śrīmad Bhāgavatam*, the Mahajana Yamaraj uses the same term (*paro dharmaḥ*) in declaring that the twelve Mahajanas, the supreme authorities on religion, are unanimous in agreement that devotion to Krishna is the highest religion and that it begins with chanting the Holy Name of Krishna.

etāvān eva loke 'smin
puṁsāṁ dharmaḥ paraḥ smṛtaḥ
bhakti-yogo bhagavati
tan-nāma-grahaṇādibhiḥ

"The ultimate purpose of existence is to love God, Krishna. The path of devotion begins with chanting his Holy Name."

Thus anyone who is fortunate enough to become fixed in the true activity of the soul is fit to be placed on the highest seat in human society, more worthy of respect than Brahmins or anyone else.
(*Śrīmad Bhāgavatam* 6.3.22)

Krishna tells Uddhava that according to one's individual proclivity one is categorized as a karma yogi, jnana yogi, or bhakti yogi, but without bhakti, no one can attain the supreme destination. Thus, the other yoga systems are dependent on bhakti, while bhakti is dependent on none. Krishna goes on to tell Uddhava:

na sādhayati māṁ yogo
na sā khyaṁ dharma uddhava
na svādhyāyas-tapas-tyāgo
yathā bhaktir-mamorjitā

"O Uddhava! Neither eightfold yoga, philosophy, the study of scripture, austerities nor renunciation can help one to attain me. But I am a slave to impassioned devotion." (*Śrīmad Bhāgavatam* 11.14.20)

Bhakti, service saturated with love, is most adored by the Lord. He says:

"Knowledge and renunciation are not considered of any benefit to the fortunate yogi whose heart naturally flows towards me and who is united with me in love. Whatever benefits he could obtain in this world by work, austerity, education, renunciation, mystic yoga, altruism, religion, or any other apparently auspicious path, he attains easily through his devotion.

"My devotees can have whatever they want — life in the heavenly planets, Brahman realization, even admittance into Vaikuntha — but since they love me dearly, they even refuse to accept my offer of liberation from the cycle of birth and death." (*Śrīmad Bhāgavatam* 11.20.31-35)

Why are the desires for liberation and sense gratification called the deepest darkness of ignorance, the greatest self-deception and unnecessary for the soul? And why is Krishna prema the utmost necessity and the prime human goal? Even the sharpest of pandits, after extensive study of Vedanta, cannot answer these questions. Thus Krishna Das Kaviraj Goswami has written:

"According to our karma we are wandering in the world aimlessly. Only the most fortunate souls find a real guru by the mercy of Krishna. And by the mercy of the guru, the seed of devotion is carefully planted in one's heart. Then, like a vigilant gardener, the devotee cares for it, watering it with Krishna's name and acts of devotion.

"As the *bhakti-latā-bīja* (the seed of devotion) grows, it gradually becomes a creeper that penetrates the covering of this material universe, extending into the spiritual world. It grows beyond the *brahma-jyoti* and enters the *para-vyoma*, or spiritual domain. Finally it reaches the highest spiritual realm of Goloka Vrindavan and entwines itself around Krishna's lotus feet, which fulfill all desires. There it bears the fruit of prema love of God. Even though the gardener lives within the world, he continues to nourish the creeper with Krishna's name and service.

"However, if by chance the devotee commits Vaishnava aparadh, it is like letting a mad elephant loose in his garden of devotion. This offense will uproot his bhakti creeper and destroy it. Therefore, the gardener must build a protective fence around his creeper of devotion and avoid committing Vaishnava aparadh.

"The other threat is weeds choking the creeper. The desires for sense pleasure, liberation and numerous other mundane desires are weeds. Duplicity, violence in the form of meat-eating and the desire for fame and fortune, are all weeds that will choke the creeper.

"These weeds thrive by sapping the energy spent in nurturing the *bhakti-latā*. Therefore the observant and introspective devotee cuts them down and protects the creeper's growth until it reaches Vrindavan. There the creeper bears the fruits of prema and the devotee reaches the lotus feet of Krishna, which are like a *kalpa-vṛkṣa* (desire-fulfilling tree). He becomes totally absorbed in tasting the fruit of prema and in serving Krishna's lotus feet. This fruit is the supreme perfection of human aspiration which makes all other goals appear tiny and insignificant."

(*Chaitanya Charitāmṛta*, *Madhya* 19.151-164)

Chaitanya Mahaprabhu revealed the esoteric principles of bhakti to Rupa Goswami and those who have realized this are indeed rare and fortunate. What could be more unfair than to persecute such a person on the basis of race, color, or social status? Everyone interested in spiritual progress must avoid Vaishnava aparadh.

Worshipping the Holy Name, Nāma bhajan, is certainly the highest form of devotion. One's level of Vaishnavism is ascertained by the depth of his absorption in Nāma bhajan. Whether one is a neophyte, intermediate, or advanced devotee—the very fact that he has committed himself to Krishna's name puts him in a position worthy of appreciation and respect. He may come from a bad background, but to judge him on the basis of any material factors is Vaishnava aparadh.

There are some points that need to be taken into consideration, however. For instance, a devotee who was born into a lower caste should not arrogantly oblige a Brahmin or someone from a higher caste to eat food that he has cooked or touched. We must not contravene Mahaprabhu's basic instruction:

tṛṇād api sunīcena
taror api sahiṣṇunā
amāninā mānadena
kīrtanīyaḥ sadā hariḥ

"One who is humbler than a blade of grass, more tolerant than a tree and ready to offer all respects to others without expecting any in return can be constantly absorbed in Krishna kirtan." (*Śrī Śikṣāṣṭaka*, Verse 3)

Failure to understand this instruction increases one's arrogance and his devotional discipline suffers. Service in the association of higher Vaishnavas should not create pride in an individual, nor cause him to consider himself a Vaishnava. This type of pride not only leads to Vaishnava aparadh but also creates an unnecessary disturbance in society.

The brilliant example of Namacharya Hari Das Thakur is worthy of emulation. Qualifying as a Vaishnava does not depend on physical strength, wealth, knowledge or social standing. Everyone must keep in mind that Krishna is generous with his mercy to the meek and humble.

Despite this injunction to always remain meek and humble, if a person witnesses an offense to a pure Vaishnava, he must vehemently protest. If he is unable to do so, with deep regret he must leave the place at once and cut off all connection with the offender. We must never minimize the seriousness of Vaishnava aparadh. Neither should we attempt to defend the offender on the basis of mundane considerations, as this will become an act of complicity that will destroy our spiritual progress and even our material well-being.

Mahaprabhu's sankirtan attracted the residents of Navadwipa

Therefore a devotee must always be extremely careful not to become an accomplice to Vaishnava aparadh. We must always remember how Lord Shiva's wife Sati went so far as to relinquish her body upon hearing offensive words about her Vaishnava husband.

Just as thinking oneself to be superior to others is a character flaw, so too is the kind of affliction associated with the "inferiority complex." If one becomes depressed thinking that he is inferior, that is not helpful to his spiritual progress. Both of these extremes interfere not only with the achievement of genuine Vaishnava qualities, but even of attaining the minimum requirements of human life.

A person is recognized as a Vaishnava only when he has established himself in Sri Chaitanya Mahaprabhu's teachings. He must live by the following verse found in the *Padyāvalī* of Rupa Goswami. It is so important that it also appears in *Śrī Chaitanya Charitāmṛta*:

nāhaṁ vipro na ca narapatir nāpi vaiśyo na śūdro
nāhaṁ varṇī na ca gṛhapatir no vanastho yatir vā
kintu prodyan-nikhila-paramānanda-pūrṇāmṛtābdher
gopī-bhartuḥ pada-kamalayor dāsa-dāsānudāsaḥ

"I am not a Brahmin or a king. I'm not a businessman or a member of the working class. In fact, I don't identify with any class. I'm not a monk; I'm not married. I'm not retired. All I am is an insignificant servant of the servants of Krishna who, resplendent with the highest pleasure, is an endless reservoir of nectar who takes care of his gopis."

(*Chaitanya Charitāmṛta Madhya* 13.80)

When Vaishnavas born to higher-class families look down on those born in the lower-classes, then they do not even understand common courtesy, what to speak of proper Vaishnava etiquette. On the other hand, the scriptures also forbid embracing Vaishnavism so that one can pass judgment on Brahmins. Verbal attacks on Brahmins by so-called Vaishnavas, and vice-versa, can only degrade societal values. There is nothing spiritual about such conflicts; they only lead to chaos and disruption.

One of the most absurd examples of aparadh took place in Krishna's lila: Once, a king named Paundraka claimed that he was Vasudeva, Krishna. He sent a message to Krishna in Dvaraka that he should either step down from his position as God, or face him in battle. Upon hearing such ravings, Krishna laughed and sent the reply that if Paundraka did not stop this insanity he would have to face the consequences. The Lord followed up on his threat, killing both Paundraka and his ally, the King of Kashi. To pretend that one is Krishna is the height of insolence and leads to doom; similarly, posing as a Vaishnava while being intoxicated with pride is disastrous.

The final decree of Mahaprabhu is not just the renunciation of bad association or the giving up of our social designations. He says that though the renunciate and the surrendered soul have similar characteristics, the devotee not only gives up the world, but also offers himself to the Lord. A devotee takes complete shelter in Krishna with full dedication. This is the culmination of surrender—*ātma-nivedana*.

If one's renunciation lacks soul-surrender, then gradually it becomes superficial and false. False renunciation (*phalgu-vairāgya*) invites the ghost of impersonalism to attack the intellect.

This *Bhagavad-gītā* states:

viṣayā vinivartante
nirāhārasya dehinaḥ
rasa-varjaṁ raso'py asya
paraṁ dṛṣṭvā nivartate

"We may refrain from sense enjoyment, but the taste for it remains. Only by experiencing the higher taste of bhakti rasa do we become fixed in higher consciousness." (*Bhagavad-gītā* 2.59)

This means that as one increases his commitment to Krishna consciousness, automatically his attachment to mundane concepts and identities diminish. At the same time, Vaishnava qualities blossom in his character to a commensurate degree. Such a fortunate soul

Swayam Bhagavan-Sri Sri Radha & Govinda

has not only the twenty-six virtues attributed to Vaishnavas, but virtues that are unlimited in number. The *Chaitanya Charitāmṛta* says that a devotee of Krishna is decorated with Krishna's qualities. When a devotee develops love for Krishna, he loves everything connected to Krishna (*kārṣṇa*) and surrender to Krishna's lotus feet becomes his only interest. This is true sadhana and bhajan.

As the devotee begins to identify himself as the servant of the servants of Krishna, bad association resulting from identification with the body begins to disappear. Pure attraction for Krishna and *kārṣṇa* awakens. There is no room for envy and pride in the heart of someone who has reached this state of consciousness. He no longer feels impelled to self-promotion or self-aggrandizement. The heart's yearning to seek Krishna intensifies to the degree that the devotee sincerely cries out Krishna's name day and night. Everything else fades into oblivion.

Therefore, pure Vaishnava theology has nothing to do with either attachment or excessive hostility to one's social position. A natural indifference to one's social status arises by following the pure Vaishnava religion of service to Krishna and *kārṣṇa* through the process of complete surrender formulated in Mahaprabhu's teachings.

If a person from the lower rungs of society desires the respect of a Brahmin and outwardly accepts Vaishnavism as his religion, then his spiritual pursuit is materially motivated. Materialistic motivation does not equate with pure Vaishnavism. It is a grave offense to treat a Vaishnava as a non-Vaishnava or to judge him by mundane standards, but it is equally offensive to praise a non-Vaishnava and worship him as a Vaishnava, or to glorify a neophyte devotee as an advanced devotee.

Only when one is fixed in the Krishna conception in his inherent spiritual identity and is devoted to Krishna and *kārṣṇa* under the direction of Sri Guru can he find relief from the clutches of Vaishnava aparadh. Our predecessor acharyas have warned us that our chanting will never become pure if we keep bad association; at best such chanting is only mere shadow of the pure name or *nāmābhāsa* and *nāmāparādha* is always lurking. Bad association is always a detriment to the path of Krishna bhakti. So if one desires to chant Krishna's name purely he must associate with Vaishnavas. Simultaneously, he must stop craving carnal pleasure, liberation, mystic power and other material things.

bhukti-mukti-spṛhā yāvat,
piśācī hṛdi vartate
tāvad bhakti-sukhasyātra
katham abhyudayo bhavet

"There is no question of experiencing the pleasure of devotion as long as the twin ghosts of sense pleasure and liberation haunt us."

(*Bhakti-rasāmṛta-sindhu* 1.2.22)

According to spiritual authorities, *asat-saṅga* is comprised of non-Vaishnavas. They are karmis (sensualists), jnanis (empiricists) and mystics, whose real desire is to achieve power. Advancement in bhakti is directly connected to avoiding bad association and seeking and keeping good association.

The predominant quality of a Brahmin is *sattva-guṇa* (the mode of goodness). The Kshatriyas (governing class) are under the influence of a strong *rajo-guṇa* (passion), mixed with a weak *sattva-guṇa*. The Vaishyas (businessmen) are controlled by a mixture of *rajas* and *tamas* (passion and ignorance), while the Shudras (working class) are predominantly in the clutches of *tamo-guṇa* (ignorance). So the Brahmins are considered to be the highest class in human society because they are endowed with noble qualities like sense control, truthfulness and the ability to discriminate between matter and spirit. They are the gurus or spiritual guides in the Varnashram system of social order.

In the ancient Vedic social stratification there are four spiritual orders of life, or ashrams: those of the brahmachari or celibate student, the householder, the *vānaprastha* or retired person and sannyasi or renunciate. Of these, sannyasa (renunciation) is preeminent because it facilitates freedom from mundane entanglement, thereby making it easier to elevate oneself to the transcendental plane. However, Kaviraj Goswami is quick to warn those who think that the sannyasa order gives a person special status:

"If the followers of the Varnashram system simply observe the regulations and responsibilities of their social and religious orders but neglect to worship Krishna, they fall into a degraded condition."

The *Śrīmad Bhāgavatam* states that: "The followers of the Varnashram system who neglect the worship of Lord Vishnu become arrogant and obsessed with their social positions and fall down."

(*Śrīmad Bhāgavatam*, 11.5.3)

The most important quality of a devotee is that he serves Krishna, indifferent to what or who is superior in this material world. The scriptures state that devotees of Krishna are the most elevated members of society, whereas non-devotees are degraded regardless of their social position. In order to worship and serve Krishna, material qualifications are not necessary — everyone is eligible.

The *Śrīmad Bhāgavatam* makes constant reference to the fact that work without devotion is useless. The same principle applies to education, philosophy, yoga, or anything else. Pure devotion is above and beyond devotion mixed with karma, jnana or yoga.

Those who understand the true meaning of these statements in the scriptures are beyond any social restriction. However, this cannot be used as an excuse to not follow the rules and regulations of devotion.

"As long as one has not awakened a taste for devotion, he is obliged to adhere to the regulative principles of the Vedic injunctions." (*Śrīmad Bhāgavatam*, 11.20.9)

A faithful devotee is not inspired by any activity other than devotion because hearing Krishna's wonderful pastimes has aroused his faith. According to the degree of his surrender, he will ignore the social order (Varnashram). At the same time he realizes the need for establishing a structure to keep society from falling into a state of anarchy and chaos.

Deviations from the Vedic injunctions are the bane of modern society. Plagued by uncontrolled and irresponsible habits in diet and sex, the ideals and benefits of the Varnashram system have been for the most part lost, even within India. The erosion of the moral standards that govern all human interaction should alarm anyone who is concerned with the ultimate good of human society. Vaishnavas cooperate with persons who are like-minded and have similar habits, but they cannot support the present-day society's capriciousness and, more importantly, its apathy to God consciousness.

In the pursuit of devotion even one's eating habits are important. It has been said, "You are what you eat." The eightfold yogic system also prohibits a yogi from accepting food cooked by persons with mentalities contrary to their own. Such food causes wavering of resolve in those who desire to elevate themselves in yoga and may yield a disastrous result. Regulations in every aspect of preparing and taking food directly affect the levels of purity in one's consciousness. The Vedas say:

āhāra-śuddhau sattva-śuddhiḥ,
sattva-śuddhau dhruvānusmṛtiḥ

"When one follows a pure diet, the consciousness is also purified and this makes it possible to focus the mind in constant remembrance of the ultimate goal of life."

(*Chāndogya Upaniśad* 7.26.2)

For this reason, strict devotees won't even accept food cooked by Brahmins if they are non-devotees. In the *Itihāsa-samuccaya* the Lord says:

"A person who has no devotion is not dear to me even if he is learned in all the Vedas, but if a reformed meat-eater performs devotional service then he is dear to me. Therefore one should give charity to such a person and receive gifts from him, for he is as worshipable as I am."

(*Hari-bhakti-vilāsa* 10.127)

Devotees relish prasad, or food offered to the Supreme Lord with love and devotion, and never refuse prasad from any Vaishnava regardless of his family background. Such refusal is another form of Vaishnava aparadh. If ever a question arises about whether or not to follow the scriptures or social custom, we should follow the example given us by previous authorities, the spiritual master or those who are close to the spiritual master. But in whatever situation we find ourselves, we must always be particularly careful not to allow a disrespectful attitude to the Vaishnavas enter our hearts. There is no worse obstacle to our advancement in spiritual life.

Srila Raghunath Das Goswami has shown that our spiritual life is not limited to the cultivation of Krishna consciousness. He writes in his *Manaḥ-śikṣā*:

"My dear mind, my brother, I humbly bow before you and beg you to please give up all pride and surrender fully to Sri Gurudeva, to the spiritual abode of Vraja Dham, to the residents of Vraja, to all the Vaishnava devotees of the Lord, to the Brahmins, to the holy name of the Supreme Lord and to the ever youthful Divine Couple of blossoming beauty, Sri Sri Gandharvika Giridhari, and in this way quickly develop sublime attachment to them."

Srila Raghunath Das Goswami addresses his own mind in order to speak to us and his teachings are indispensable to our spiritual progress. A Vaishnava must remain prideless like Raghunath Das. Even though he was fully conversant with the esoteric conclusions of pure devotion, he exemplified proper Vaishnava conduct. Even if a Vaishnava is very elevated, he always thinks of himself as lowly and meek. We must constantly remember Mahaprabhu's instruction of *tṛṇād api sunīcena*, that we should feel humbler than a blade of grass. If one thinks of himself as an elevated Vaishnava then he cannot remain prideless. The desire for fame and adoration (*pratiṣṭhā*) will contaminate his consciousness. If he purposely leaves his food remnants for others, his consciousness will become weighed down by arrogance. In order to avoid these pitfalls, the Vaishnava must always think of himself as the humble disciple of his spiritual master who is simply accepting worship on his guru's behalf.

Once the devotee is able to feel himself to be an insignificant servant, then nothing will divert him from the path of *śuddhā bhakti*. His heart will always shine with humility and there will be no room for the darkness of deceit. To feel pride internally while making a show of humility is dishonest and absolutely foreign to a pure devotee.

One who has developed pure love for the Supreme Lord, who is immersed in meditation on the Holy Name, whose heart is constantly searching for Krishna while sincerely crying out to him — such a person is undoubtedly a Vaishnava who can purify the entire world. He has achieved the characteristics of a devotee mentioned by Krishna in the Gītā: he is *nirdvandva,* free from indecision and doubt, *nitya-sattvastha,* fixed in his own spiritual identity, *niryoga-kṣema,* free from the worries of accumulation or bodily maintenance, and *ātmavān,* self-possessed. Under no condition does pride, honor, or even worship affect him. Offering obeisances to everyone, whether animal or outcaste, as part of Krishna, is for him a perfectly natural mode of behavior. He spontaneously follows Vrindavan Das' dictum:

ei se vaiṣṇava-dharma sabāre praṇati
dharma-dhvajī jāra ithe nāhi rati

"This is the essence of the Vaishnava religion — to bow down before every living creature. One who has no taste for such behavior is a hypocrite."

(*Chaitanya Bhāgavata* Antya 3.29)

According to this exalted standard, a Vaishnava will never insult even an ordinary jiva, what to speak of another Vaishnava! He is the embodiment and the protector of Mahaprabhu's teachings:

jīve sammān dibe jāni kṛṣṇa adhiṣṭhān

"Offer respect to all living beings knowing that Krishna resides in their hearts."

Sri Sri Radha-Gopinath jiu

If we can emulate such an elevated mood, then by the Vaishnavas' mercy, we can acquire the great fortune of relishing the nectarean ocean of pure devotion.

[1] Parankush Muni is a name of the greatest of the twelve Alvar saints of the Śrī Sampradaya. He is otherwise known as Sathakopa or Nammalvar.

[2] These categories are particularly well known in the Śrī Sampradaya. Pillai Lokacharya has spoken of them in his *Śrī-vacana-bhūṣaṇam*.

[3] These distinctions are also well known in the Śrī Sampradaya, going as far back as the Pañcarātra Āgamas.

Sri Nityananda Prabhu

Spiritual Suicide
Guru Aparadh

SRILA KAVIRAJA GOSWAMI MOVINGLY describes the disappearance of Srila Madhavendra Puri in *Śrī Chaitanya Charitāmṛta*. At that time one of his disciples, Ramachandra Puri, saw that his guru was chanting the Holy Name and weeping, crying out "*mathurā nā pāinu*," which means, "I could not attain Mathura." Madhavendra Puri was actually exhibiting symptoms of *vipralambha-bhāva*, or the mood of intense separation.

Ramachandra Puri was by nature a faultfinder, and consequently could not receive Sri Guru's grace. Although he was Madhavendra Puri's disciple, his vision was warped and he saw his guru as a mundane person. In utter disregard of the transcendental status of his guru, he said: "Just remember that you are Brahman and therefore full of transcendental bliss by nature. You should know this, so what are you crying about?"

Madhavendra Puri was enraged at his disciple unabashedly giving him such dry philosophical instructions. "Get out you sinful rascal. I don't want to see your face!" Then he began to lament, "O Krishna, I could not reach you, nor your abode, Mathura. I am dying in unhappiness, and this rascal comes to give me even more pain. I am dying without your shelter and now this fool comes to instruct me about Brahman." Ramachandra Puri was rejected by his guru and thus material desires gradually appeared in his heart.

Srila Bhaktivinoda Thakur elaborates on the meaning of the word *vāsanā*, or "desire" in his *Amṛta-pravāha-bhāṣya* commentary: "Here, 'desire' indicates attachment to knowledge and analysis, which ultimately leads to Vaishnava aparadh. The real cause of a jiva's misfortune is his offenses against guru and Vaishnava."

We learn more about *vāsanās* in Krishna Das Kaviraj's account of the Lord's conversion of Prakashananda Saraswati. When in Benares, Mahaprabhu would take his bath in the Ganges at the Panchanada and then visit the Bindu Madhava temple as part of his daily routine. At the temple he would sing the names of the Lord and dance with his devotee companions. One day while he was thus engaged in kirtan, Prakashananda Saraswati came by with a large number of his sannyasi followers.

This meeting took place after Mahaprabhu had purified Prakashananda of his distorted impersonal understanding of spiritual life and the great philosopher had surrendered to the Lord. He asked the Lord again and again to forgive him for the offenses he had committed in the past due to his ignorance of the devotional path. When Mahaprabhu assured him that his past sins had been forgiven, Prakashananda said,

"Previously I had insulted you. Now that I have

Srila Prabhupada Bhaktisiddhanta Saraswati Thakur

touched your lotus feet, all these offenses have been washed away. The *Vāsanā-bhāṣya* states that desires for material pleasure or *vāsanās* can awaken in even liberated souls (*jīvan-mukta*) if they commit offenses to the Lord who possesses infinite and inconceivable powers.

"You are the Supreme Lord himself and yet you think of yourself as the Lord's devotee. In either case, you are worshipable to all of us and disrespecting you is the source of all misfortune. As Sukadeva said to Pariksit:

āyuḥ śriyaḥ yaśo dharmaṁ
lokān āśiṣa eva ca
hanti śreyāṁsi sarvāṇi
puṁso mahad-atikramaḥ

"Committing a wrong to a great soul shortens one's lifespan, destroys one's reputation and spiritual principles, and puts an end to all the blessings one has received. Indeed, all that is good in one's life come to an end as a result of such offenses." (*Śrīmad Bhāgavatam* 10.4.46)

Jiva Goswami finds support for the idea that a liberated soul (*jīvan-mukta*) can become entangled again in material desire and the consequences of his actions if he does not remain fixed in bhakti yoga (*Bhakti-sandarbha* 110).

The term used here, *jīvan-mukta*, is defined in the *Nāradīya-purāṇa* as follows:

īhā yasya harer dāsye
karmaṇā manasā girā
nikhilāsv apy avasthāsu
jivan-muktaḥ sa ucyate

"One whose mind, body and words are engaged in the service of the Supreme Lord at every moment of his life, whatever the circumstances, is said to be a liberated soul even while living in this world, or *jīvan-mukta*."

So the above statements make it clear that even such a *jīvan-mukta* can fall down if he offends a Vaishnava. Fall down means becoming attached to money, sex life and personal prestige.

The impersonalists often use the word *jīvan-mukta*. Indeed, they often consider themselves to be liberated. In fact, however, no one who is devoid of devotion to Krishna has pure consciousness. Thus the Lord says to Sanatana Goswami that the jnanis only think they are liberated, but that in fact their minds are still polluted due to the absence of devotion. Thus, however elevated they may become, these jnanis always fall down, as the *Bhāgavatam* says, "due to neglecting the Lord's lotus feet."

If one commits offenses to the Lord himself, then offenses to the Lord's devotees inevitably follow. And if one commits offenses to the Lord's devotee, one calls down the Lord's anger on himself.

This is what happened to Ramachandra Puri: he had the audacity to offer instructions to his guru — a *mahā-bhāgavata* who personified Krishna prema. He failed to understand that his guru was immersed in *viraha*, or separation from Mathura, the transcendental abode of Krishna.

Srila Bhaktisiddhanta Saraswati Prabhupada writes in his commentary: "Realizing that his disciple was a fool, Madhavendra Puri withdrew his connection with and any responsibility for him."

Once Ramachandra Puri had been rejected by his guru, it was inevitable that he should become a hardened critic of Vishnu and the Vaishnavas. This unfortunate soul once went to visit Mahaprabhu in the Gambhira temple in Puri. While waiting, he saw ants crawling outside Mahaprabhu's door. Without thinking, Ramachandra Puri said, "Last night there was sugar candy here and therefore ants are everywhere. Alas, this sannyasi is attached to sense gratification."

After saying this, Ramachandra Puri got up and left. He continued to take an interest in the Lord's every activity, inquiring after his habits, how much he ate and slept, and what he did. When he found nothing blameworthy in the Lord's habits, he went back to the accusation that the Lord was eating sweets: "Chaitanya has taken the renounced order of life and yet eats sweetmeats of various kinds. How can he expect to control his senses if he permits himself the pleasures of the tongue?"

Ramachandra continued to visit Mahaprabhu every day, but his only objective was to find fault with the Lord and then to publicly broadcast his criticisms. Reports of these false accusations eventually reached the Lord. Indeed, Ramachandra Puri was not afraid to speak his mind directly to the Lord.

Despite such behavior, Mahaprabhu always followed Vaishnava etiquette and offered Ramachandra Puri the same respect due his own spiritual master, Ishvara Puri, because he was his spiritual master's godbrother. He thus accepted Ramachandra's criticism of his eating habits and even changed his diet. He told his servant Govinda: "From now on it will be a rule that I shall accept only one-fourth of what I have been eating of Jagannath's prasad. If you bring any more than this, I will leave."

When Govinda disclosed Mahaprabhu's self-imposed austerities to the Lord's other intimate followers, they felt as if the world had ended. That day a Brahmin came to offer Jagannath prasad to Mahaprabhu. Acting on Mahaprabhu's orders, Govinda accepted only one-fourth of a pot of rice and vegetables. Mahaprabhu then took only half of that amount and left the other half for Govinda. The Brahmin was horrified.

"My love, My heart is upset and agitated because I can't see You. What do I have to do to see You again? You know that I am helpless, please be kind to Me!"

Seeing Mahaprabhu eating so little, the devotees were overcome with despair and stopped eating altogether. Mahaprabhu, however, ordered his servants Govinda and Kashisvara Pandit to beg food from somewhere else to compensate for their smaller portions. This continued for a few days and finally the news reached Ramachandra Puri, who came to see Mahaprabhu. Mahaprabhu received him with due honor, offering him obeisances and a seat. Ramachandra Puri laughed and instructed the Lord:

"It is not the business of a sannyasi to gratify his senses. He should fill his belly somehow or other. I heard that you have cut down your eating by one-half. I can see that you have become skinny. Such dry renunciation is also not the religion of a real sannyasi. A sannyasi eats only as much as necessary, but he does not try to please the senses. If you act in this way, you will soon attain the perfection of jnana yoga."

Mahaprabhu, the exemplar of humble and respectful behavior, replied: "I am just an ignorant boy and like your disciple. It is my great fortune that you instruct me."

Ramachandra Puri left, and Mahaprabhu learned that the devotees were either fasting completely or had reduced their eating by one-half for many days. Then one day a group of devotees led by Srila Paramananda Puri came to meet Mahaprabhu. Paramananda humbly said to the Lord:

"My godbrother Ramachandra Puri is by nature a critic. If you give up eating because of his faultfinding, what will you gain? He encourages one to eat to his full satisfaction, and then to eat more than necessary. Then, after he has induced one to overeat, he defames him saying, 'You eat too much. How much money do you have? By setting a bad example for other sannyasis, you ruin their vows. It's easy to understand why you have not made any spiritual advancement.'

"Ramachandra Puri always is always trying to find out what people are doing and how much they are eating. He has made it his duty to follow two kinds of activities rejected in the scriptures. It is written in the *Bhāgavatam*: 'One should see this world as being under the control of Krishna and neither praise nor criticize the characteristics and activities of others. One who praises or criticizes others is trapped in duality, and soon deviates from the ultimate goal of life.'

"Of these two rules, Ramachandra Puri obeys the first: he never praises anyone. And although he knows that the second is more important, he continues to criticize others."

Srila Bhaktisiddhanta Saraswati Prabhupada writes in his *Anubhāṣya* commentary:

"In the *Bhāgavatam* we find that 'to not praise' is the first rule, and 'to not criticize' is the second. If the second rule is given prominence over the first, then the conclusion is that it is not so bad to praise, but it is imperative not to criticize. Ramachandra Puri observed the first rule, but he failed to adhere to the second."

Srila Paramananda Puri continued: "A slanderer like Ramachandra does not consider a person's virtues, even if he has them by the hundreds. Rather, he attempts to cleverly turn these virtues into faults. But it is not enough to merely avoid Ramachandra Puri's example. Something should be said against him because he is breaking our hearts. Please don't give up eating on account of this fool."

Chaitanya Mahaprabhu replied: "Why are all of you angry at Ramachandra Puri? He is simply stating the standard principles of sannyasa life. Why condemn him? For a sannyasi to overindulge in the pleasures of the tongue is a great offense. The duty of a sannyasi is to eat only as much as is needed to keep body and soul together."

After this, the devotees fervently requested that the Lord resume his normal eating habits. At first the Lord refused, but later agreed to take only half of his original portion instead of a fourth.

The Lord's custom was to take a specified amount of Jagannath prasad, which was provided by the contributions of two or three devotees each day. Certain closer associates were allowed to supplement this prasad with food they had cooked at home. The Lord is subjugated by his devotee's love for him, thus on days when Gadadhar Pandit, Sri Bhagavan Acharya, or Sarvabhauma Bhattacharya invited him to dinner, he had no choice but to eat as much as they gave him. The Supreme Lord is like a desire-tree and would submissively accept prasad according to the devotee's desire. The prime reason for the Lord's descent is to give pleasure to his devotees. The Supreme Lord always acts in ways he deems appropriate to the time and circumstances. Kaviraj Goswami writes:

"Because of the absolutely independent position of the Divinity, Mahaprabhu sometimes acted like a common man and sometimes he manifested his godly opulence. Sometimes the Lord accepted Ramachandra Puri as his master and considered himself his servant, and at other times he would ignore him, as though he were no more significant than a speck of dirt. Although it may baffle our intelligence, we must remember that God can do anything he likes, and whatever he chooses to do is always irresistibly charming."

After staying in Nilachala for a few days, Ramachandra Puri left for pilgrimage. With his departure, the devotees felt as if a heavy burden had been lifted from their heads. Relieved and happy, they resumed enjoying prasad to their full satisfaction. The Lord himself once again filled himself with the bliss of kirtan and dancing. Kaviraj Goswami concludes:

"If one's guru rejects him, one becomes so fallen that he commits offenses even against the Lord. Chaitanya Mahaprabhu did not take Ramachandra Puri's offenses personally, for he considered him to be on the level of his guru. However, through his behavior, the Lord taught everyone about the risks of offending the guru."

In complete contrast to Ramachandra Puri, total devotion to the guru is exemplified in the life of his godbrother Ishvara Puri, the guru of Chaitanya Mahaprabhu. Ishvara Puri personally served Madhavendra Puri, knowing that he was a pure devotee of the Lord experiencing his *aprakaṭ a-līlā*, or pastime of leaving the body and entering the spiritual world.

Ishvara Puri personally waited hand and foot on Madhavendra Puri, even cleaning his stool and urine with his own hands, while chanting the Holy Name and recounting the pastimes of Krishna for him to relish. In this way he helped his guru to remember Krishna's holy name and pastimes at the time of his passing from this world.

Pleased with Ishvara Puri, Madhavendra Puri embraced him and gave him the treasure of Krishna prema. Ishvara Puri was filled with an ocean of ecstatic love, whereas Ramachandra Puri dried up and became a critic of everyone. Ishvara Puri received his guru's blessings, whereas Ramachandra Puri was rebuked. They are living examples of what can happen when one receives either a great personality's benediction or chastisement.

Madhavendra Puri revealed to the world the treasure of sublime love of Krishna while relishing divine love in separation (*vipralambha*). He entered into the pastimes of Sri Radha while singing the following verse:

ayi dīna-dayārdra nātha he
mathurā-nātha kadāvalokyase
hṛdayaṁ tvad-aloka-kātaraṁ
dayita bhrāmyati kiṁ karomy aham

"O Mathuranath! When will I see you again? You are supposed to be kind to the poor. I am nothing without you. Now my heart is filled with anxiety and I don't know what to do."

(*Chaitanya Charitāmṛta, Antya* 8.34)

There are four Vaishnava traditions. Madhavendra Puri accepted sannyasa in the line of Madhva. From Madhva to Lakshmipati (Madhavendra Puri's guru) this disciplic line lacked the mood of *śṛṅgāra-rasa* or erotic love. This is evident from the conversation Mahaprabhu had with the Tattvavadis (the followers of Madhva's line) during his tour of South India. Until Mahaprabhu's time the popular conception of the Absolute Truth was Vishnu bhakti, worshipping the Lord in the mood of awe and reverence.

With this beautiful verse, Madhavendra Puri sowed the seed of bhakti in *śṛṅgāra-rasa*. He became one with the mood of Sri Radhika as she experienced intense separation from Krishna after he had left Vrindavan to become a prince in Mathura. To cultivate her feelings is the highest mood of devotion. Devotees immersed in this rasa or mood consider themselves very poor and humble, and always beg Krishna to be kind to them. This is why Madhavendra addresses the Lord as *dīna-dayārdra-nātha*, "one who is kind to the poor."

Inasmuch as we are separated from Krishna, this mood is the most natural way to feel while performing acts of devotion. After Krishna departs for Mathura, Sri Radhika's heart is trembling with anxiety from not being able to see him. Yearning to behold his beautiful face, she laments:

"My love, my heart is sorrowful and agitated because I can't see you. What do I have to do to see you again? You know that I am helpless, please be kind to me!"

It can easily be seen that the mood expressed here by Madhavendra Puri resembles that of Mahaprabhu in the mood of Sri Radha in Vrindavan, especially when she saw Uddhava. Our preceptors have said that the root of the tree of *śṛṅgāra-rasa* is Madhavendra Puri; Ishvara Puri is its sapling, Mahaprabhu is its trunk, and his followers are its branches.

When Mahaprabhu went to Remuna to have darshan of the deity of Khirchora Gopinath, he recited this verse and entered the highest state of ecstasy. Krishna Das Kaviraj comments that aside from Sri Radha, Mahaprabhu, and Madhavendra Puri, no one else can relish the rasa of this verse:

"By grinding sandalwood, its aroma increases. By pondering this verse, its meaning deepens. The Kaustubha gem appeared within the cream of the ocean of milk, and this verse is the cream of all poetry because it expresses the highest concept of rasa. It is Radharani's own utterance made manifest in the world through Madhavendra Puri by her mercy. Though Chaitanya Mahaprabhu fully relished it, no one else is capable of doing so."

There is another aspect of Ramachandra Puri's relationship with Mahaprabhu and his devotees that casts light on the consequences of guru aparadh and how it grows and festers.

Sri Chaitanya performs his sankirtan lila

When Ramachandra Puri came to Nilachala, he met with Mahaprabhu and Paramananda Puri. These two naturally gave Ramachandra a great deal of respect because he was Madhavendra Puri's disciple. While the three of them were sitting together and talking, the Lord's dear companion Jagadananda Pandit courteously invited Ramachandra Puri to take Jagannath prasad as his guest. Jagadananda fed Ramachandra generously and, after he had eaten to his full satisfaction, Ramachandra encouraged him to eat. After they had both washed their hands and mouths, however, Ramachandra started to criticize his host:

"I had heard that Chaitanya's entourage was filled with gluttons, but now I have seen with my own eyes that it is true. They first try to ruin a sannyasi's reputation by overfeeding him and then they eat just as much, or more! Can a renunciate who eats this much ever remain celibate?"

This was the way Ramachandra carried on: he would first incite someone to eat more than was his wont and then would blame him for doing so. He would so shame the devotee that he could no longer lift his head.

As time went on, Ramachandra progressed with his slander from the Lord's devotees to the Lord himself. This is why it is said that if one offends the spiritual master, then it does not take long before one goes on to offend the Vaishnavas and, eventually, the Supreme Lord himself.

The Lord does not tolerate the offender of devotees; this is why such an offender is forever bereft of the Lord's mercy. Whatever acts of devotion he performs are empty and pointless, like the oblations of clarified butter on the ashes of a sacrificial fire. So everyone who aspires to spiritual life must be on his guard against committing such offenses. We do not say this to frighten you. Contemplate the example of Ramachandra Puri who began by offending his spiritual master; he then went on to commit offenses at the feet of Jagadananda Pandit and then finally his offensive attitude was directed at Lord Chaitanya

Mahaprabhu himself. Anyone who follows this contemptible path is forever bereft of an understanding of spiritual joy.

The *Śrīmad Bhāgavatam* states that remembrance of Krishna's lotus feet — meaning the eagerness to serve him — removes all inauspiciousness from our lives. In other words it removes the offensive attitude of not wanting to serve, which is the only means to attract the benediction of the Lord's grace. It awakens in the jiva's heart the desire to serve the Lord. Through service, he is freed from mundane influences and becomes situated in pure goodness or *viśuddha-sattva*. Unalloyed devotion for the Lord dawns in his heart as he relinquishes his slavery to the material modes. He naturally becomes detached from things unrelated to Krishna and receives the highest grace. But by blaspheming Sri Guru and the Vaishnavas, all is forfeited and destroyed.

By offending a devotee who has taken shelter in the Holy Name, the taste for chanting disappears. One hovers on the material plane of consciousness plagued by desires (*vāsanās*) that bring misfortune and inauspiciousness. The real benediction for everyone has been nicely delineated in *Śrī Chaitanya Charitāmṛta* in the discussion between Mahaprabhu and Srila Ramananda Raya.

Ramananda Raya says that devotion to Krishna is the ultimate realization in transcendental knowledge. The highest fame anyone can achieve is being a devotee of Krishna. The most precious possession is divine love for Srimati Radharani and Sri Krishna, and the greatest suffering is separation from Krishna's devotees. A lover of Krishna is the most exalted, liberated person. Ecstatically singing about the sublime pastimes of Radha and Krishna is the highest religion. The association of Krishna's devotees is the only real good for everyone. Krishna's transcendental name, qualities, beauty, and pastimes, are the only subjects worthy of constant remembrance, and the lotus feet of Sri Radha and Krishna are the only things we should worship and adore.

The only place worth living is Vrindavan. There, Radha and Krishna revel in their divine dance of love, the Rasa lila. The eternal pastimes of Radha and Krishna are the only topics worth hearing. The singing of the holy names of the Divine Couple is the highest form of kirtan and the most exalted form of worship. This is real culture and should be the ultimate goal of human civilization. But if aparadh against Hari, guru, and Vaishnava infect the heart, then we digress from the spiritual path and are dragged onto the miserable path of hedonism.

"My dear devotees, I humbly beg all of you, please! Do not commit Vaishnava aparadh"

Bharatavarsha, India, is the doorway to the spiritual world, Vaikuntha, where gods and goddesses compete to take birth as humans—a birth that offers the best opportunity for association with Vaishnavas and a service connection with Krishna. That precious gift is destroyed by aparadh and one's life becomes a burden.

Chaitanya Mahaprabhu descended from the innermost quarter of the transcendental abode of Sri Radha and Krishna to remind us of our actual identities as their eternal servitors. But if we allow our innate nature to become diverted from serving Radha and Krishna, becoming slaves of illusion, the rare opportunity offered by the human birth is wasted.

" The worship of My devotees

is the real worship of Me.

In fact it is higher than

worshipping My very Self.

One can chant the Holy Name

birth after birth, but if one

is chanting with offenses, he will

never love Krishna or experience

a taste for the Holy Name."

Gaura-Nitai

The Most Merciful

The Supreme Lord Krishna manifests himself in the material world in four forms as the Vaishnava, Tulasi, the Ganges, and *Śrīmad Bhāgavatam*. The deity form of the Lord becomes worshipable only after it has been consecrated ritually and the Lord's presence has been invoked. These four things, however, are innately sacred."

(*Chaitanya Bhāgavata Madhya* 21.81-82)

Srila Bhaktisiddhanta Saraswati Prabhupada comments on this verse in his *Gauḍīya-bhāṣya* commentary: "The Lord appears in the material world in these four forms. Upon seeing them, it is not immediately evident to ordinary people that they are the Lord himself. However, because of their intimate connection with him, they are called his *prakāśa-vigraha*, or visible manifestations.

"Generally people think that the deity form of the Lord is only worthy of worship after being formally installed (*prāṇa-pratiṣṭhā*). These four *prakāśa-vigrahas*, however, are considered to be naturally worshipable; there is no need for any kind of ritual in order to elevate them to that status. They are to always be considered distinct from the material nature and never looked upon as potential objects of sense enjoyment. Rather we should look upon them as in the position of the enjoyer, or *bhoktā*, as the master or *prabhu*, and as bestowers of divine grace and knowledge."

"Mahaprabhu himself says, 'Those who worship me directly but neglect my devotees are in illusion and cause me pain. Their offerings feel like a shower of burning cinders on my body. Just because one is chanting is no guarantee of success. I destroy anyone who tries to hurt my devotees:

je āmāre dāsera sakṛt nindā kare
mora nāma kalpa-taru saṁhāre tāhāre

"If someone blasphemes my servant even once, then my name will destroy him rather than fulfilling his desires."

(*Chaitanya Bhāgavata Madhya* 19.209)

"In fact, everyone and everything in this universe is my servant. Therefore someone who acts enviously and violently to other living beings is bound for destruction. Even a sannyasi who blasphemes a devotee who has no hatred in his heart for anyone falls down from his position and his religious principles."

Mahaprabhu, bright with his effulgence of golden light, raises his arms in the air and proclaims to the world, "Give up criticizing Vaishnavas and take shelter of the Holy Name!

anindaka hai je sakṛt kṛṣṇa bhaje
satya satya muñi tāre uddhāribo hele

"Verily I say that I will immediately deliver anyone

Worshipper

who, free from the faultfinding tendency, worships Krishna, even for just a moment."

(*Chaitanya Bhāgavata Madhya* 19.214)

If one offenselessly chants Krishna's name even once, then Krishna will liberate him from material bondage. However, a person may be well-versed in all the Vedas, but if he still maintains an offensive attitude towards the Vaishnavas, he is eternally doomed. Is it any surprise, then, that we often hear people say, "Although I have been chanting for years, I have no taste"?

Srila Prabhupada writes in the *Gauḍīya-bhāṣya*: "When one stops his offenses against the Vaishnavas and utters Krishna's name even once, he easily receives the Supreme Lord's grace. Criticizing the sadhu is the same as criticizing the lotus feet of Sri Guru, and that is an offense against the Supreme Lord. Gradually degrading to the level of *bhagavan-nindā*, an offender of the Supreme Lord is not only deprived of receiving prema, but due to his *nāmāparādha* he does not even come anywhere near achieving the benefits of religion, wealth, or material enjoyment."

Kaviraj Goswami reminds us: "There are offenses to be mindful of when approaching *kṛṣṇa-nāma*. Offensive chanting never brings about the desired change of heart.

tad-aśma-sāraṁ hṛdayaṁ batedaṁ
yad gṛhyamānair hari-nāma-dheyaiḥ
na vikriyetātha yadā vikāro
netre jalaṁ gātra-ruheṣu harṣaḥ

"If by vibrating the holy name of Krishna our hairs do not stand on end, our eyes do not flood with tears, and there is not a volcanic eruption of ecstasy in our bodies, our hearts must be covered in steel."

(*Śrīmad Bhāgavatam* 2.3.24)

It is written in the *Chaitanya Charitāmṛta* that, "Simply vibrating the name of Krishna once destroys all sin and then devotion gradually develops into love, Krishna prema. When the heart is saturated with prema, it pounds, the body sweats and shivers, speech

falters, and the eyes are flooded with tears. When we take the name of Krishna in the mood of divine service, so much wealth is gained that the struggle for existence is over without our even trying. However, if one repeatedly takes the name of Krishna and is not moved to tears, it is obvious that aparadh is preventing the seed of *kṛṣṇa-nāma* from sprouting."

Then what is our recourse? Kaviraj Goswami says that in chanting the name of Krishna, there is the consideration of offenses, but in chanting the names of Mahaprabhu and Nityananda Prabhu, the most magnanimous manifestations of Divinity, there is no such consideration.

"If one chants the names of Mahaprabhu and Nityananda Prabhu with even a little faith, he is immediately cleansed of all offenses. Then when he chants *kṛṣṇa-nāma*, he feels ecstasy. Sri Chaitanya Mahaprabhu is unlimitedly magnanimous. Without worshipping him, what hope is there for liberation?"

This does not imply that Mahaprabhu and Nityananda Prabhu bestow prema in the presence of aparadh. They are so magnanimous that whoever seeks shelter at their lotus feet receives their mercy. Soon the offenses disappear and the offender feels love for Krishna.

Bhaktivinoda Thakur says: "If we surrender to Mahaprabhu and Nityananda Prabhu, all our previous offenses are instantly absolved. Then the merciful Holy Name showers us with divine love."

Bhaktisiddhanta Saraswati Thakur writes: "Krishna and Gauranga are their names, and their names are their very selves. To consider Krishna inferior or less generous than Gauranga is ignorance. But the fact is, Gauranga and Nityananda are especially helpful to the fallen souls in achieving the goal of life. The more the jivas become fallen, the more merciful the Lord becomes. Gauranga and Nityananda are the ultimate manifestation of divine kindness, and within that kindness is found the sweetness of Krishna's pastimes.

"Nevertheless, worship of Gauranga does not exclude the worship of Krishna, nor does it mean exclusively worshiping Mahaprabhu without seeing him in terms of Sri Radha and Krishna. That kind of so-called devotion is fictitious, and is devoid of even a drop of the divine nectar of Krishna prema."

Mahaprabhu never tolerated Vaishnava aparadh. Ramachandra Puri, Devananda Pandit, and others are vivid examples of this truth. Even Mother Sachi had to beg forgiveness from Advaita Acharya before the Lord would bless her with prema. Only when one sincerely approaches the offended Vaishnava and begs forgiveness will he be forgiven. Then offenses disappear; otherwise the consequences are fatal. As long as the heart is covered by offenses it is impregnable.

Bhaktivinoda Thakur sings:

Krishna's generosity is confined to the liberated, the perfected yogis and those who have already taken shelter of him. Gauranga Mahaprabhu and Nityananda Prabhu, on the other hand, are so kind and generous that they take the most unqualified souls, free them from the offenses that come of the selfish enjoyment mentality and, after liberating them, give them a place at the feet of Gaura-Krishna.

"Offenses have made my heart as hard as steel and as cruel as thunderbolts. O Lord, even your Holy Name has no effect on it. I feel hopeless and helpless, O Lord, so I loudly cry your Holy Name.

"O Gaura! O Nitai! You two brothers are friends of the fallen. I am the most fallen, wicked person and you are oceans of mercy. So please save me!"

This is the critical difference between Krishna lila and Chaitanya lila. Sri Krishna Das Kaviraj Goswami concludes the *Madhya-līlā* of *Śrī Chaitanya Charitāmṛta* with this secret revelation:

kṛṣṇa-līlāmṛta-sāra
tāra śata śata dhāra,
daśa-dike bahe jāhā haite
se caitanya-līlā haya,
sarovara akṣaya
mano-haṁsa carāha tāhāte

(*Madhya-līlā*, 25.271)

"Krishna lila is the cream of all nectar, only the confidantes of Sri Radha and Krishna and the eternally perfect souls can enter there. So how then should we conceive of Chaitanya lila? The pastimes of Sri Chaitanya Mahaprabhu are an infinite reservoir, from which thousands of streams of the nectar of Krishna lila are flowing in all directions, inundating everyone everywhere. May the swan of my mind swim there eternally, and dive deep into its infinite waves of nectar."

tad idam ati-rahasyaṁ gaura-lilamṛtaṁ yat
khala-samudaya-kolair nādṛtaṁ tair alabhyam
kṣatir iyam iha kā me svāditaṁ yat samantāt
sahṛdaya-sumanobhir modam eṣāṁ tanoti

(*Chaitanya Charitāmṛta Madhya-līlā* 25.283)

"Gaura lila is deeply mysterious and confidential. It is the secret to devotion and love of Krishna. Those who are envious of Krishna and his devotees are like animals unable to taste its nectar. But I do not lament having described Mahaprabhu's lila because nothing is lost. Rather something is gained, because those devotees who are pure of heart expand the līla by tasting and relishing it again and again."

Pujyapad Srila Bhakti Promode Puri Goswami Maharaj

Vaishnava Sarvabhauma Sri Srila
Bhakti Promode Puri Goswami Maharaj

In the early years of this century, Srila Prabhupada Bhaktisiddhanta Saraswati Goswami Thakur set into motion a devotional revival that rapidly spread through Bengal, India, and eventually the world. He put into question the very foundations of present-day theistic thought in a way that has little comparison anywhere in the spiritual record, East or West. Through him, the world was awakened to the teachings of Sri Chaitanya Mahaprabhu and the movement of pure devotion, śuddhā bhakti.

In orchestrating this modern bhakti revolution, Srila Prabhupada gathered some of the greatest spiritual luminaries in contemporary history into his circle. Such a convergence of exalted spiritual personalities can only be compared to the coming together of Sri Chaitanya's direct followers in the sixteenth century. One of the devotional giants who entered Srila Prabhupada's orbit was the author of this book, His Divine Grace Srila Bhakti Promode Puri Goswami Maharaj.

We cannot describe the life of Srila Puri Goswami Maharaj without emphasizing his contribution to the spiritual movement in which he was so integrally involved. The depth of his accomplishments cannot be fathomed outside the context of Sri Gaudiya Math. With his fellow godbrothers, he shared an indomitable faith in the service of his Guru and the message of Sri Chaitanya Mahaprabhu. This service was the sole purpose and highest aspiration of his being. This conviction led him to spend his entire life in the pursuit of Srila Prabhupada and Mahaprabhu's pleasure and the fulfillment of their desires. If we examine his life in this setting, we will see more than just numbers, dates, places and names. We will see how he embodied the very life current that his spiritual preceptors came to give the world.

Srila Puri Goswami Maharaj took birth in the village of Ganganandapur in Jessore district (in present-day Bangla Desh), on October 8, 1898. His parents, Tarini Charan Chakravarti and Srimati Ram Rangini Devi, named him Sri Promode Bhushan Chakravarti. During his childhood, he met his vartma-pradarśaka guru ("one who opens the door to the path of devotion"), Srila Bhakti Ratna Thakur, a godbrother and siksha disciple of Thakur Bhaktivinoda, the legendary architect of the present Gaudiya Vaishnava movement. Through Bhakti Ratna Thakur he was introduced to Sajjana-toṣaṇī, Bhaktivinoda Thakur's own Vaishnava periodical, which was filled with Bhaktivinoda's commentaries and holy teachings. In this way Srila Puri Maharaj became familiar with the seminal works of the śuddhā bhakti tradition, such as Chaitanya Charitamrita, Chaitanya Bhagavata and the

Srimad Bhagavatam. It was also through Bhakti Ratna Thakur that he first learned of his future guru, Srila Bhaktisiddhanta Saraswati Goswami Prabhupada.

Srila Puri Maharaj was still a young university student when he first came before Srila Prabhupada at the Yoga Pith in Sri Mayapur in 1915. It was a significant occasion, for Srila Prabhupada's diksha guru, Paramahamsa Thakur Srimad Gaura Kishor Das Babaji, had entered his eternal abode only the day before. Srila Puri Maharaj often recounted that as soon as he saw Srila Prabhupada and paid his obeisances to him for the first time, he knew in his heart that this was his spiritual master. Some years later, on the auspicious day of Sri Krishna Janmastami in 1923, he accepted both Harinam and mantra diksha from Srila Prabhupada and was given the name Pranavananda Brahmachari.

At the time, Sri Gaudiya Math was rapidly establishing itself as a bona fide manifestation of Indian religious culture and transforming the caste-conscious socio-religious world of Hinduism. Srila Prabhupada Saraswati Thakur was bringing together his intimate associates to share the wealth of Sri Krishna sankirtan. He had accepted tridaṇḍī sannyāsa in 1918 and by the early 1920's had already assumed a formidable position in the Bengali spiritual firmament. He was fearless when it came to upholding true religious principles. The students and practitioners of the Gaudiya Math aligned themselves with this attitude and led most exemplary lives of devotion, imbued with austerity, discipline and in-depth scriptural learning. This high standard of religious life was the hallmark of Sri Gaudiya Math and would be the thread that guided all of Srila Prabhupada's disciples, including Srimad Puri Goswami Maharaj.

The keystone of success in devotion is to perfectly hear the holy words spoken by one's spiritual preceptor. Srila Prabhupada would often say, "All that is required of you is that you lend me your ears." Srila Puri Maharaj was fully committed to this maxim. He had the great good fortune to associate closely with Srila Prabhupada for thirteen years and during that time he served him personally by recording his lectures and conversations, which were later published. The greater part of Srila Prabhupada's spoken words we are left with today come from the transcriptions of these notes. At the same time, Srila Puri Maharaj cultivated a deep knowledge of the Vaishnava scriptures, with the result that he became a veritable storehouse of the wealth of the preceptorial line coming from Sri Chaitanya and his followers. This led him to become one of the most prolific writers and influential teachers in all of Gaudiya Vaishnava history. His writings reflect the disciplined eye of a scholar who expresses with grace and directness the purest scriptural conclusions supported by his own uncommonly profound realization.

Following Srila Prabhupada's directives, our Gurudeva edited, wrote for, published and helped distribute countless spiritual publications. He was initially inspired and directed by Srila Prabhupada to start writing and contributing articles to the Gauḍīya magazine, the backbone of the Gaudiya Math's missionary work. For seven years he served as a proofreader and as one of its primary editors. In 1926, he was charged with running the world's only daily Vaishnava newspaper, Dainika Nadiyā Prakāśa. He held this service for two years, publishing all of his preceptor's daily discourses along with articles by fellow students and other contemporaries. His service and learning did not pass unnoticed by Srila Prabhupada who awarded him the titles of mahā-mahopadeśaka ("great instructor") and pratna-vidyālaṅkāra ("keeper of the wisdom of the ancient scriptural lore").

After the disappearance of his Gurudeva in 1937, Srila Puri Maharaj continued his vocation of spreading the teachings of Sri Chaitanya through the Gauḍīya magazine, first out of the Bagh Bazaar Gaudiya Math and then later the Sri Chaitanya Math in Mayapur. After he founded the Sri Chaitanya Gaudiya Math, Srila Puri Goswami Maharaj's godbrother, Srimad Bhakti Dayita Madhava Maharaj, invited him to head the editorial board of Chaitanya Vāṇī magazine in 1964. Puri Maharaj served in this capacity for thirty-three years, furthering his life's work of preserving the teachings of his spiritual lineage. Through Chaitanya Vāṇī, he continued to make a deep impact on the devotional world.

In all, our venerable teacher's wisdom is embodied in over sixty years of writings on Vaishnava philosophy and theology. He penned a rich variety of texts, bringing the Bhagavata dharma to life through hundreds of poems, essays, narratives, diaries, editorials and personal letters, thus creating a storehouse of the wealth of pure devotion for his disciples and the world at large.

In 1942, Srila Prabhupada appeared to Srila Puri Maharaj in a dream vision and imparted to him the sannyas mantra, ordering him to accept the renounced order. After accepting tridaṇḍī-sannyāsa from his godbrother Bhakti Gaurava Vaikhanasa Maharaj in Champahati in August of 1946, he toured parts of India with other godbrothers such as Bhakti Hridoy Bon Maharaj and Bhakti Dayita Madhava Maharaj. In the meantime, he continued to write and lecture with dedication. At the behest of his godbrother Tridandi Swami Bhakti Vilasa Tirtha Maharaj, he also served for seven years as chief pujari for the Yoga Pith temple, the birthsite of Sri Chaitanya Mahaprabhu.

Srila Puri Maharaj took up a more solitary life of worship in the 1950's. He moved to a humble cottage on the banks of the Ganges in Ambika Kalna. The king of Burdwan was extremely impressed by his saintly ascetic character and, on the appearance day of Srimati Radharani in 1958, presented him with the ancient Ananta Vasudeva temple in Kalna.

In 1989, at the age of 91, Srila Puri Goswami Maharaj established the Sri Gopinath Gaudiya Math in Ishodyan, Sri Mayapur, for the service of their divine lordships, Sri Sri Gaura-Gadadhar, Jagannath Deva, Radha-Gopinath and Lakshmi-Narasingha Deva. In the following years, he established other temples in Jagannath Puri, Vrindavan, Calcutta and Midnapore.

Srila Puri Maharaj taught through his every action. He excelled in all aspects of devotional practice and there was perhaps no area in which he did not exhibit utmost expertise, diligence and foresight. This ranged from his encyclopedic knowledge of scripture, to maintaining the printing press, to his beautiful singing of kirtan. He was especially recognized for his sensitivity and attention to detail in the performance of deity worship and devotional rites and was thus widely called upon to be the head priest in most of the Gaudiya Math's deity installations and ceremonial functions. He was rarely known to rest; his service was an uninterrupted flow. Even in his later years, he would remain awake, writing and chanting through the night while all his youthful disciples were still asleep. When his personal servants came in the morning, they would inevitably find him awake and chanting the Holy Name, arisen before everyone else in the ashram.

Srila Bhakti Promode Puri Maharaj had outstanding love for his godbrothers and was inspired in his glorification of others. He found richness in everyone he met. He had the quality of making one feel so much wanted and their life so much valued. At the same time, he paid the least attention to himself. He was an emblem of humility and simplicity, and his generosity of spirit and kindness touched the hearts of the whole Vaishnava community. Among his lifetime, intimate companions were Srila Bhakti Rakshak Sridhar Deva Goswami Maharaj, Srila Bhakti Prajnan Keshava Maharaj, and Srila Akinchan Krishna Das Babaji Maharaj. Toward the end of his sojourn in this world, he was honored by the Gaudiya Vaishnava community for his learning, long life of service and devotion and made president of the World Vaishnava Association in 1995.

"He has love for his Guru; and let it be known that his life is one with his words." This tribute, coming from Srila Prabhupada himself, is the most revealing statement about Srila Puri Goswami Maharaj's personality and qualities. He gave credit for all of his accomplishments to the mercy of his Gurudeva alone. Through the blessings of Srila Bhaktisiddhanta Saraswati Goswami Thakur, Srila Bhakti Promode Puri Maharaj attracted the hearts of so many to the Bhagavata religion. People from so many different backgrounds and countries found in him a true spiritual guide and shelter. He upheld the principles of pure Vaishnavism and delineated the path of śaraṇāgati. He so embodied pure devotion and service to his spiritual master that one of his disciples once remarked that he was able to "silently lay down Srila Prabhupada's entire siddhanta."

We are greatly indebted to His Divine Grace for his gift–a lifetime of pure devotion, spanning over a century, which we can aspire for, learn from, and discuss about for our own spiritual nourishment. Srila Puri Maharaj departed this world for the eternal abode in the predawn hours of Narayan Chaturdasi, October 21, 1999, one day before the Rasa Purnima. His divine body was transported from Jagannath Puri to the Gopinath Gaudiya Math in Ishodyan and there placed in his eternal samadhi shrine. Prior to his departure from this world, Srila Puri Goswami Maharaj appointed his intimate disciple, Sripada Bhakti Bibudha Bodhayan Maharaj as his successor and President-acharya of Sri Gopinath Gaudiya Math.

In years to come as more of his words and vision are translated, the world outside of Bengal and India will come to know the spirit of the true Vaishnava religion that he tirelessly shared. May the gentle rain of nectar of his perfect teachings continue to bring auspiciousness into this world.